RED HOT INTERNET PUBLICITY

An insider's guide to promoting your book on the Internet

Penny C. Sansevieri

For more information, contact info@amarketingexpert.com.

ISBN: 1480224952
ISBN 13: 9781480224957

MORE BOOKS BY PENNY C. SANSEVIERI

Nonfiction

Get Published Today (Wheatmark, 2012)

52 Ways to Sell More Books (Wheatmark, 2012)

Red Hot Internet Publicity (Cosimo 2010)

Red Hot Internet Publicity

(Morgan James Publishing 2007)

From Book to Bestseller (Morgan James Publishing, 2007)

Get Published Today

(Morgan James Publishing, 2007)

From Book to Bestseller

(PublishingGold.com, Inc., 2005)

No More Rejections: Get Published Today! (Infinity Publishing, 2002, 2003)

Get Published! An Author's Guide to the Online Publishing Revolution
(1st Books, 2001)

Fiction

Candlewood Lake (iUniverse, 2005)

The Cliffhanger (iUniverse, 2000)

To subscribe to our free newsletter,
send an email to subscribe@amarketingexpert.com

WE'D LOVE YOUR FEEDBACK. HERE'S HOW TO CONTACT US:

Author Marketing Experts, Inc.
P.O. Box 421156
San Diego, CA 92142
www.amarketingexpert.com

TABLE OF CONTENTS

DISCLAIMER

It is not the purpose of this book to be the single marketing tool in your library, and we always recommend the use of other books on book marketing, some of which are suggested in the references section.

Red Hot Internet Publicity contains advice on Websites, Internet marketing, promotion, and selling books. The use of this book is not a substitute for publishing, business, tax, accounting, consulting or other professional services. Consult the appropriate professionals for answers to your specific questions. Neither the publisher nor the author, or the contributors mentioned in this book, bear any liability for the incorrect or improper use of this book or the information and advice contained herein. If you do not wish to be bound by the terms of this paragraph, promptly return this book for a complete refund.

DEDICATION

To George, who once many years ago said I could.
You were right.
I miss you everyday.

ACKNOWLEDGMENTS

It would take an entire book to thank everyone involved in the process of creating *Red Hot Internet Publicity*. Of all the sections in this book, this is the most difficult to write.

There are scores of people who contribute both in their support and the willingness to share their own creativity, and there are several "behind the scenes" people who brought their own amazing level of support, information, and creativity to this book: AME's red hot girls both Paula Krapf and Amy Cornell. They are simply rock stars and, often, my rock. I thank them both for their dedication, love of this industry, creativity, wisdom, humor, and friendship. I couldn't have made it this far without both of you. Jeniffer Thompson of MonkeyCMedia, who I am lucky to call friend and who continually amazes me with her creative genius. Thanks for always making me look good and for keeping me on track, especially on the days when I felt derailed. Lauren Hidden of Hidden Helper, she is a bright and beautiful friend and an amazing editor. Lauren if you ever stop editing I will have to stop writing. Thanks for pushing me to be a better writer. Susan Gilbert of Online Promotion Success who, aside from creating our website and being an SEO whiz, is also a good friend. Susan came into my life years ago and together we've had many wonderful adventures. This journey is but one of them. I am grateful to you for your friendship and wisdom.

I am wildly fortunate to surround myself with super smart and savvy women.

There are many more people that I need to thank, and thankfully too many to list here. I am fortunate to not only be in this industry, but to be surrounded by many amazing people who always make me look so good. To them I say: Thank you. This journey wouldn't be possible without you.

To the authors who've worked with my firm and the fans who follow us and read our stuff. We love you for loving us, thanks for being so dedicated to what you do and to striving to be better.

To my friends and family who always love and support me even when my schedule doesn't always permit me to spend as much time with them as I'd like.

I have many blessings in my life. To list them all here would be endless. I continue to have a grateful heart for my work and my mission and I am enormously fortunate to be able to do what I love. I wish you the same kind of happiness.

FOREWORD

by Joan Stewart
The Publicity Hound
www.PublicityHound.com

Most of the phone calls sound the same.

An author, usually self-published, is in tears. She spent three years writing her book, and a small fortune on a book shepherd, an editor, a proofreader, a publicist, a printer, brochures, bookmarks and tchotchkes. But she still can't park in her garage. It's filled with stacks of unopened cardboard boxes of books she can't sell.

She's calling me because I'm a publicity expert. And she admits she has no clue about what she's supposed to do next.

"Who's the target market for your book?" I ask patiently.

Remarkably, she isn't sure.

"What have you already done to try to sell it?"

A speaking engagement here, she says, a book signing there. If she's lucky, a profile story in her local weekly newspaper.

When I ask for her website address so I can take a quick look, I'm not surprised to hear, "My website is horrible! Besides, I'm an author. I'm not an Internet marketer."

That one comment says it all.

When I explain that anyone who sells ANYTHING online is an Internet marketer, she mumbles something about technology being over her head. Then, she admits, "I'm lost."

More and more, "I'm lost" seems to be a common refrain among authors, speakers and business owners.

I hear it in the halls when I speak at conferences. I see the words "I'm lost" in the Q&A box when I present a webinar on how folks can use social media to market their businesses and books. I heard it again last weekend when my friend said she couldn't figure out how to get rid of her ex-husband on LinkedIn after she accidentally accepted his invitation to be a first-degree connection.

"I'm lost," she said. "That's why I don't use LinkedIn like I should."

Just when authors thought they had the world of publishing figured out and business owners were settled on how to market their businesses, along comes Internet marketing, and then the mind-numbing chore of social media.

Enter Penny Sansevieri.

If marketing online was a 1,000-piece jigsaw puzzle, Penny would be the one you'd want sitting next to you at the kitchen table. She's an author, a business owner, a publicist and a marketing expert who helped create 11 best-sellers in 22 months. Rather than grabbing a fistful of pieces, she'd help you create a strategy for tackling the online marketing puzzle. Jigsaw puzzle junkies say it's easiest to pick out all the pieces with straight edges and build the frame first. Penny agrees. Even before you think about marketing your products or services, she'd want you to build the frame. That is, a list of your all-important keywords--words and phrases, all tied to the topic of your book or focus of your business, that you'll use in your marketing to pull traffic to your website.

Then she'd help you gather together the inside pieces of the puzzle that look like they belong together--step-by-step instructions on how to build your website, tips on how to use words at your website, and advice on how to turn your website into a sales machine--so you could start assembling the puzzle in chunks.

Days later, when all the oddly shaped, interlocking puzzle pieces are in place, the completed picture of how to market online would finally make sense. Build the puzzle correctly and you'll finally hear "ka-ching! ka-ching!"

But you can't have Penny next to you. That's why you need this third edition of Red Hot Internet Publicity--an insider's guide to promoting your book, online.

If you're thinking about marketing online, read Red Hot NOW, before you spend another minute online. It will put you miles ahead of all the other business owners, speakers and authors who are calling me for help, months after their books are published or their businesses launched. Penny will keep you from making the same incorrect assumptions others made. Costly errors, they later discovered, turned into marketing nightmares.

If you've already written your book or been at your business for a while, her help will be invaluable because it can jump-start sagging sales.

Here's what I like best about Red Hot: It's written for the non-techie newbie who I sometimes fear is being left behind by the Internet marketing mentors and the social media gurus. While they're teaching about Facebook's Edgerank score, and how to measure your conversion rate from Facebook traffic at your website, folks who don't know a Facebook profile from a Facebook page are telling themselves, "I'm lost."

Penny *assumes* you are. That's why she starts with the basics like the most popular search engines and how to choose a domain name. You'll find simple worksheets and must-do checklists that help you keep the puzzle pieces well organized as you do things like hire a web designer and determine what the key messages will be at your site.

Gradually, she will introduce you to more technical aspects of Internet marketing and explain in drop-dead simple terms things like how to analyze your web traffic and create autoresponder campaigns for email marketing.

Red Hot is also a valuable reminder for experts like me who have been doing Internet marketing for 15 years. In the chapter on "Search Engine Optimization Tricks," I had a half dozen of those slap-my-palm-on-my-forehead moments. For example, when I use Craigslist to advertise my rental property, I'm inundated with calls. So why am I not using it, as Penny recommends, to get sign-ups for my ezine and let people know about my new ebooks and special reports?

As for social media, this third edition does two important things: It gives an overview of the most popular sites for building a community and marketing your books, and explains specific steps you should take to market.

Determine which sites will give you the best traction *and which you most enjoy*. I love LinkedIn and Twitter, but have been tempted repeatedly to bail out of Facebook. Struggling with its never-ending changes isn't my idea of fun. And then there's Penny, whose Facebook page boasts more than 75,000 fans, and you can tell she's having a ball. Different strokes for different folks.

Finally, who better than Penny, creator of the Virtual Author Tour™, to explain why you need to blog, how to blog, and how to pitch bloggers. They can help you sell far more books than a book reviewer in a major newspaper.

Red Hot is a quick, easy read that scanners will love. Pay attention to all the "Red Hot Tip!" boxes scattered throughout the book. Pick and choose which chapters you need most. Or, if you're new to Internet marketing, read it all the way through without taking notes so you can get a good idea of what the finished puzzle will look like. Then go back and make a to-do list of only three tasks. Tackle them all, and then make a new list of three more things, and so on.

If you know the types of people who are ideal buyers for your book or consumers for your business, but you don't know how to use the technology to find them, you're in luck. Red Hot shows you how.

UNDERSTANDING INTERNET PUBLICITY

"I think there is a world market for maybe five computers."
— Thomas Watson, IBM Chairman, 1943

Recently, I was called upon to explain Internet publicity to a group of people who knew very little about the Internet or publicity. I started talking to them about traditional publicity such as press releases, ad placement in newspapers and talk show appearances, even though the first two items are practically extinct. After ten minutes of talking, I could see that my point was falling on deaf ears. Then, a couple of ideas occurred to me. Before I totally lost my audience, I threw it out there and hoped for the best. Here is the gist of what I said:

In a recent episode of *Deadliest Catch*, the crew places cameras on Alaskan king crab boats, documenting the crews as they travel far out to sea in search of prized king crab. When they get to a good spot, they sink a huge, bait-filled metal cage to the sea floor, leaving a buoy behind to mark the spot. Several days later, the boat comes back and retrieves the cage, hoping to find it loaded with expensive crab.

When thinking of the Internet, I want you to understand that the crab cage and bait is your website. You put it up and wait for the crabs to come. Hopefully these visitors become your eventual clients and you will entertain them at a Red Lobster King Crab Feast night.

What I have just described is a *passive* form of advertising on the Internet. Put your site out there and hope they come. The next type of Internet publicity is *active* advertising. To explain this I am going to talk about a book I read recently that is now also a movie: *The Hunger Games*. The main character is a young girl who is lethal with a bow and arrow. In the story, she finds a bunch of arrows and stores them in her quiver. Then she stalks her prey, shooting an arrow into it with deadly accuracy when she finds it. This is very much like Twitter, Facebook, blogging and email newsletters. These are arrows in your quiver, and you have to spend time actively engaging your prey to gain publicity.

Whether you use the "drop the crab cage and wait for them to come" approach, the "stalk them with a bow and arrow" method or both, you are the captain of your ship. You get to decide which arrows you will use and when to use them. That's what Internet publicity is all about: using the available tools and techniques for promoting anything.

It's a Brand New Day

When the first glimmer of Internet publicity entered the world of PR, most authors thought it was boring. I mean, how exciting could it be to pitch yourself to a blog or newsgroup? There were no cameras; heck, there wasn't even a microphone. But in the case of bloggers, their power has taken over. Some bloggers have been known to get as many readers as a daily newspaper. Instapundit, a blog run by Glenn Reynolds in his spare time, has more incoming links than *Sports Illustrated*'s SI.com.

The advent of blogging, tweeting, pinning, podcasting and other Web 2.0 "citizen generated media" has created a long tail of media drivers. The further we get down this tail, the more we find that the television programs we would have traded a kidney for in the past are not even skimming the surface of the media that really drives readers to products, people, books and, consequently, sales. The idea of Internet publicity isn't just publicizing yourself on the 'Net, it's getting into peer groups with solid, focused messages that match yours. And it's about creating your momentum online by going after online media, regardless of whether the blogger is with MSNBC or the Boomer Women of America's website. As long as it's in your topic, and it isn't a mom and pop "here's what we're having for dinner" type of site, you may be close to striking Internet gold.

How to Use This Book

Throughout this book you will learn the latest tips, secrets and best practices to get you maximum publicity. First a word about all this information: Please don't be overwhelmed. If you just want to start with Chapter Two: Social Media, that's fine. I started there because it's easy to use and free. If you just mastered that chapter, you are bound to gain a ton of publicity for your company, book, website or whatever you are promoting. Once you have used as many social media tools as you desire, then move on to the next chapters. If you are someone who can absorb it all fast, then by all means rip through it. If you forget something, don't worry, it will always be there for you to refer back to at any time.

Now go forth and multiply your message.

PART ONE:
RED HOT SEARCH ENGINE OPTIMIZATION

Warning: the Internet may contain traces of nuts.
— Author Unknown

SEARCH ENGINE OPTIMIZATION TRICKS

Yesterday it worked
Today it is not working
Windows is like that
— Haiku by Margaret Segall

Trying to get Google, Bing and Yahoo! to notice you? Well, there might be a solution. As we describe in this book, there are a variety of ways to get a higher listing in Google. The ideas in this chapter are elaborated on later in this book, so let's highlight them here. It may not soar you to the top of the search engine ranking, but it will definitely help you in your quest for better ranking.

Red Hot Tip!

For a quick listing in Google, head on over to: http://www.smartzville.com/google-homepage.htm **and submit your site!**

Getting Your Site Listed in Search Engines

A search engine can't produce your site in a search result if it doesn't know about it. You can wait until the search engine finds your site or you can take matters into your own hands by submitting it yourself to the search engine. You can list your website with search engines in a number of ways: (a) pay a service to do this for you; (b) do a mass submission yourself; or (c) list your site individually at each search engine. Although (c) is the more tedious of the processes, it might be worthwhile to consider. Remember, if you make one mistake when mass submitting your site, it could take months to correct.

Mass Submissions

A mass submission is when you access hundreds of online search engines through a promotion site (like AddMe.com, for example). The site will take you through the steps of submitting once you have completed its application form. Be wary of this. While it worked for my site, it also submitted my link to FFA's (Free For All's) and I ended up on about a hundred mailing lists. Here are some mass submission sites:

- Free Web Submission (www.freewebsubmission.com) – will mass submit your site to 50 search engines.
- AddMe.com – has dozens of free services to help drive traffic to your site.
- Submit It! (www.submit-it.com) – used to be free, now has some elaborate packages to choose from.

When using the sites, read the fine print of your agreement. Most of them are free and a great time-saver, but they can cost you in other ways.

Individual Submissions

Now let's talk about individual submissions. When you opt to submit your site to individual search engines, you are essentially hand submitting to all these sites yourself. While this may seem like a lot of work (it is), it could be worthwhile. You can focus on submitting to the most popular sites (listed below), and then add sites as you come across them, or as you feel they are relevant.

Popular Search Engines

- Google.com
- Bing.com
- Yahoo! (www.yahoo.com)
- Ask.com
- AOL.com
- MyWebSearch.com
- Lycos.com
- DogPile.com
- WebCrawler.com
- Info.com

Premium Directory Listings

List yourself in the best directories. You'll have to pay for this, but because most people don't do it (since everyone's looking for a freebie), you could really enhance your traffic by getting a listing at Yahoo! Directory (dir.yahoo.com), Business.org or Best of the Web (www.botw.org). If you are feeling adventurous, try DMOZ.org. It's not easy to get listed there, but it's worth the effort.

What's a Site Map and Why Would You Need One?

Search engines send out little robotic critters called spiders that track down websites. Once a spider gets on your site, it follows all the links and (hopefully) indexes all the pages on your site. If you have a site map, spiders can hit that and then scurry out to all your other pages, helping your chances of getting the entire site indexed. And the more pages that get indexed, the greater your chances of having your site land in someone's search.

If you have a huge site, site maps also help your site visitors find what they're looking for faster. But the truth is, visitors rarely use these. Site maps are typically done for search engines to aid in optimization and give them even more great content to link you to.

Ease of Navigation

Driving traffic to your website is only good if they stay awhile and browse. Too many websites make it hard, if not impossible, to get around the site and see what all is there. When you design your site, make sure your designer understands the importance of having a simple, clean navigation. It will make a huge difference in user satisfaction and, ultimately, traffic.

Are You Trustworthy?

As you work to increase your page ranking, one of the factors that major search engines take into consideration is trustworthiness. Sound silly? It's true. Google is looking to provide their customers with the same level of value that you offer yours. One way to do this is to include a privacy policy on your site. This shows that you are serious about providing a valuable service to your users and that you have integrity and a sense of responsibility. Also, placing a physical address and telephone number on your site tells Google that you may actually be a legitimate business. This *trust* issue is becoming a huge factor with Google.

Red Hot Tip!

Research has found that people innately trust well-designed sites much more than poorly designed ones; a site that seems trustworthy will gain more links and traffic. Research credit: Northumbria University

Become a Resource of Information

While some SEO tricks involve computer programming or html knowledge, others are much simpler. Content is one of them. On the Internet, content is king, so make sure your site has great content. Write articles and blogs. Believe it or not, this is an incredible tool for driving traffic. Well-written, relevant articles can net quite a bit of activity to your website. And while I used to be a fan of pushing articles and content to article sites, the age of Google has diminished that marketing tool.

Most search engines love a high volume of quality content. The more you have on your site, the more likely you are to show up higher in the search engine ranking. A study from search engine marketing company Medium Blue found that search users are up to six times more likely to click on the first few organic results than they are to choose any of the paid results. They also discovered that for PPC (pay per click) ads, the overall conversion rate, or the rate at which searchers take a desired action on a site, is 17% higher for unpaid search results than for paid (4.2% vs. 3.6%).

The trick then is to post fresh new content as frequently as you can. When you don't keep adding to your site via page additions or blog postings, your site will sink in results.

Bookmarking

Social bookmark *everything*—and I do mean everything. You can bookmark each page of your site and each blog entry you post. While this might seem tedious, it's worth it. You'll see a strong increase in traffic if you social bookmark each page on your site and each of your blog entries.

Social Networking

Set up a social networking page with Facebook, LinkedIn or Google Plus. It's free and easy to do. Just don't forget the all-important link back to your site!

Delicious

Create a "recommended by" list on your Delicious (formerly De.lico.us) page. You can do this by logging on and creating an account at www.delicious.com and then tagging articles, blogs and other content you think is important to your readership. Then offer this page as a resource site. You can add a link to this page in your email signature line or on your website.

Yahoo! Answers

Lend a helping hand. Start answering questions at Yahoo! Answers (answers.yahoo.com/). You don't have to spend hours on there, but maybe a few minutes a week. Make sure to include a link back to your site following your answers.

LinkedIn Groups

We'll discuss this more in the LinkedIn chapter, but for now keep these groups in mind; they can be a great place to post content and drive more users to your site.

Craigslist

Offer a freebie on Craigslist.org. You'll be amazed at how much traffic you get from a single Craigslist ad. The key here is to send people to a page on your site and make sure they have to sign up for something (like your email newsletter) before they can grab their freebie. That way you're not just getting traffic, you're also building your list.

eBay Store

If you have products to sell, why not get a store on eBay? This site gets a tremendous amount of traffic, and on your sales page you're allowed to list your URL. It's another great way to get an inbound link and a way for people to find you. Here are a couple of interesting articles on the importance of eBay for sales and backlinking:
http://www.techiewww.com/marketing/top-5-sites-you-must-get-backlinks-from
http://www.internetretailer.com/2012/01/18/us-sales-ebay-grew-10-q4

Podcasting

Podcasting is another great way to drive traffic. Start a podcast by going to Audio Acrobat (bookmkr.audioacrobat.com/—yes, this is our affiliate link). There are other programs you can use, but I love this one because you can record the podcast over the phone quickly and easily and then hit the "send" button on your computer once it's recorded. The system will syndicate it to twenty-seven podcast directories including iTunes. It's a great way to let people know about you and your website!

Video

Load a video on YouTube. If you don't have a video or don't know how to create one, contact us and we'll refer you to our fabulous video people.

Incoming Links

Google (aka controller of the Internet) loves incoming links, but the trick is they must be high-quality and relevant. Don't squander your time (or a perfectly good link) on smaller low-traffic sites. Go after sites, blogs and online magazines and offer them an original article, or comment on their blog postings. Good sites should have a PR (PageRank) of 4 or above depending on the market. You can find out what a site's PageRank is by downloading the Google toolbar, which comes with a PR feature built in. All of these links will get spidered in Google—and voila! Welcome to the wild world of SEO.

About Outbound Links and Resource Pages

It's true that outbound links do not help much when it comes to SEO, but they are still a good thing. Here's why: search engines are looking to see if you are offering something of value on your site. Chances are if you offer outbound links, Google will see that as a good thing. Every little bit helps.

A good place to have outbound links is on a resource page. Just be sure the links open in a new window so you do not lose your visitor. And be careful not to send them away from your index page.

Resource pages are also a great way to give your visitors added value, as long as the links indeed offer something useful. Also, remember to check your site for broken links at least once a month. Broken links affect how search engines index your site and can hurt your PageRank. Here's a free tool to check for broken links: www.brokenlinkcheck.com/. Your webmaster should run regular tests as well.

Newsletter

Start an email newsletter. While it may not seem like this would drive traffic to your site, you'd be surprised at the effectiveness of this type of promotion. If your newsletter (like your articles) is interesting and relevant to your audience, you'll find that it has a huge pass-through factor, meaning that it is passed from one email subscriber to another. Also, if you have an email newsletter you should never, ever go to a single event without your handy signup sheet. Yes, you can even use offline events to drive traffic to your website. I will talk more about newsletters in a later chapter, but know that for driving more traffic to your site, it's a winner.

Interviews

If you're ever quoted in a magazine or other publication, make sure to mention your URL when it's appropriate to the topic. Don't be too pushy about this, but remember to tell folks you have a website that may be a great resource for the topic of your interview.

Signature Line

Add a signature line to your email promoting your product, service, book and website. And speaking of your email signature line...do you have one? If you don't, create one. Believe it or not, people do follow these links. You'll be amazed how many folks read email signatures. I have one and change it several times a year, depending on what we're doing or promoting or what books I have coming out.

Traffic Numbers

Make sure you know your traffic numbers—how many people are visiting your site—before you launch into any Internet marketing campaign. You want to know this so you can gauge a before and after view of your marketing efforts.

The Human Touch

It used to be that search engines like Google used algorithms to determine the relevance of your site's content. Consequently, it has been an uphill battle to determine what they place the most importance on and how to get your name higher in the ranking. This trend is slowly changing, with search engines moving to a hands-on approach that integrates a human editorial process. What this means is that offering valuable content will increase your ranking: the more value your site offers your client, the more kudos you will get from Google. Don't be afraid to give things away, including information. Remember this: Google wants their customer—the searcher—to have the best experience. That means the searchers must *find* what they are looking for. If your site provides a great experience for the searcher, he or she will be back and Google will see that. Thus, you will be ranked higher and higher.

Quick and Dirty SEO Tricks

Here are some easy ways to optimize your site without even trying:

- Make sure that your product or book has your URL on it.
- Make sure your URL is on your business card.

- Whenever you're doing an event or talk, have handouts that clearly list your URL, and maybe even give them a special bonus (like a free report) for going to your site.

- Add keywords to the header of your site (this is called metatags).

- Check out your Internet stats (often called an analytics report) to see what keywords people are using to find you, and then incorporate them into your metatags.

Conversion

If you're going to go through all the trouble of getting traffic to your site, make sure it's converting this traffic into something useful. Get folks to sign up for something—your newsletter or the RSS feed on your blog. Whatever it is, getting their email address will help you remarket to them when the time is right. Studies show that visitors landing on a site often don't buy the first time. That's okay! You want to get them into your marketing funnel so you can market to them again and again—not in a way that's obtrusive, offensive or downright annoying, but in a way that is helping them with their own mission.

An example of this might be an email newsletter. A blog is another great way to keep people in your marketing loop without bombarding them with "please buy my stuff" messages. The bottom line is that if they visit your site, get their email address.

PART TWO:
YOUR WEBSITE

"A journey of a thousand sites begins with a single click."
— Author Unknown

BUILDING YOUR WEBSITE

"SUPERCOMPUTER: what it sounded like before you bought it."
— *Anonymous*

Why You Need a Site

When it comes to websites, some people still wonder if they even need one. I mean, you have a Facebook account, right? Who needs a website? It's just another thing to manage.

I like to compare having a website to having a fax machine. These days most of us don't give a fax machine (or a document scanner) a second thought. Years ago, everyone in business had a fax machine and some people just owned them for personal use. But when fax machines first came out, I remember wondering, "Who in the world would use a fax machine?" Well, as it turns out, everybody. Fax machines became a sign of credibility. Now the website has been added to the list of credible things you can do to build your own selling empire, and for a variety of reasons you shouldn't use your social media page as your website. Here are few more reasons why you should have a website:

- Have a 24/7 sales tool.
- Create a network of supporters, fans, readers.
- Promote your events/products/ideas.

- Make yourself available to the media.

- Social media sites like Facebook change constantly, and since we can't control the changes or what will be popular among your fan base, your website is your homebase—you control it, and ultimately sites like Facebook will drive traffic back to your site.

There are businesses that can get by without a website, though candidly there aren't many of those. Before you decide, I recommend that you conduct some online research first. Figure out who your competition is in your market. Find out who's doing what, who's selling what and what their websites consist of. This research will not only help you get to know the competitive market, it will also help you determine what you like and don't like about other websites that are selling or promoting the same product or service.

Researching Your Marketplace

Whether you're trying to determine if you need a site or if you just want to get a sense of what your competition is doing, the research is fairly simple. You'll want to head on over to your favorite search engine and plug in the keywords or phrases that describe your product, service, book or brand. Keep in mind that different search engines will produce different results, though that doesn't necessarily mean you need to use several search engines during this stage of the process. Right now we're not looking for ranking, we're just gathering data. Searches across the 'Net will vary greatly depending on the platform you use to search, though the heavy-hitters in your market will tend to rank consistently high. This means that sites may rank differently or, in some cases, not show up at all.

As you start to dig into the various sites, it will be important to define your searches so you aren't just "surfing," you're researching. For each site you peruse, gather the following information:

- Website address (URL)

- What you like about it (keep this to five points per site—eventually you will see a pattern emerge)

- What you don't like about it (same for this one—five points)

- Products, services, books and other e-commerce items for sale (if your competitors sell something other than your competing product, take note of this—it could be valuable later on)

- Contact points (for networking, to email the owner to find out the name of their web designer, etc.)

I recommend starting with the top ten sites within your market. You don't need to look at every single site (eventually we'll get into competition research), for now just get a sense of what's out there. After you have that research done, sit down and look at everything. Make a list of the pros and cons of having a website. Then decide.

What Exactly Does "Building a Site" Mean?

Building a website, like a foundation to a house, has many stages. "First," says Jeniffer Thompson of Monkey C Media, "you need branding and a working concept. The only way to build a firm foundation is to know your audience. This will help you build something that will engage your customers and draw them in. Once you have a focus, you can start designing your concept. The final stage is the programming stage. I recommend that your designer and your programmer be two different people. It is best if your team works in the same office or has experience working together. A designer is an artist and does not typically think in terms of 'code,' while a programmer usually has trouble designing a site that works visually. With everything, there are always exceptions."

Defining Your Goals

It's important to define what your exact goals are before you engage a web designer. A web designer cannot help you determine your goals. It's something you need to do and then revisit often. By "revisit," I mean even after the site is up and you've had a chance to get some traffic and make some sales, you might find that your original goal for the site isn't serving you anymore. But your basic goals, the ones you start with, need to be clear and focused. You'll probably want to start with up to five goals for your site and then refine them in order of importance. We'll discuss this more later, but for now, list five goals your site should achieve:

1) ______________________________
2) ______________________________
3) ______________________________
4) ______________________________
5) ______________________________

Red Hot Tip!

Before you jump into this work, keep this in mind: the percentages of consumers who land on a site and instantly "buy" are low. Scary low. So, you want to bring them into your marketing funnel and stay on their radar screen. Hint: while one of your goals is to sell from the site, it shouldn't be your top priority. Funneling in your consumer should be high on your list and a well-designed website will help you do that.

Target Market

When we talk about defining goals, we're not talking about your needs, but rather the needs of your customer. Who is your customer? Do you have any idea? If you don't, you better get busy discovering who you're marketing to. This information isn't just important when developing your site; it's the cornerstone of all of your marketing.

Knowing your audience is also about understanding their hot buttons or emotional triggers. You'll hear me say this a lot in this book: market to someone's most pressing need and you've made a sale.

Red Hot Tip!

When you're selling aspirin, you're not really selling aspirin—you're selling pain relief. No one buys aspirin to admire the bottle; they buy it to relieve themselves of pain. Keep in mind that it's not the product or service, but the end result that we're focusing on here.

What problem does your product or service solve?

Market to a need they think about only once a week and it's going to take a lot more convincing. This is why when we talk about getting to know your customer, we call it "profiling." Creating a profile of someone you're marketing to is almost like putting together a blueprint for success. But a profile isn't something you create and then forget about. It's an ongoing effort; something that's constantly updated, amended and altered. Why? Because your customers aren't static. Their needs keep changing and evolving, and so should your website. We run a customer profile for every product we sell and we don't just do it once—we do it every ninety days. That way, while much of the information is still current, we might be able to peg a pitch on an emerging trend before everyone else catches on!

Below is a short list of questions to get you started. Generally, when I hand this list out in class, clients go home and generate several more questions on their own. The idea is that while not all of this information is relevant to the sale of your book, product or service, it will help you formulate an idea of who the person is you're marketing to. Another reason to do this is that when you know what they read (magazines) and where they hang out (clubs and organizations), it might give you a few more places to target when you launch your marketing campaign:

- Where do your customers work?
- Are they self-employed?

- Where do they live?
- Where do they play?
- What makes them happy/sad?
- What type of store(s) do they buy from?
- What magazine(s) do they read?
- What radio stations / TV programs do they watch?
- What clubs or organizations do they belong to?
- What kinds of events do they attend?
- What types of websites do they frequent?
- Would they have a website?
- Do they have a military background?
- Are they parents or grandparents? If so, will this influence their buying or surfing habits?

How Much Will All of This Cost Me?

The fees for building a website can be all over the map, with hourly rates ranging from $50 to $150. Says Jeniffer Thompson: "There are varying levels of designer fees out there, and while you could pay upwards of $10,000 to build a site, that doesn't necessarily mean that you will get the very best. A typical site should cost between $2,000 and $6,000—all of this is dependent on how large your site will be and what type of programming you will need. Flash programming costs more than basic html programming although you probably don't want Flash [more on that in a moment]."

Think of it like a car purchase—you can get your site fully loaded or stick with the standard economy class. There are also many good template sites that cost under a grand. In many cases, you do get what you pay for, especially in terms of upgradeability and search engine optimization. Ideally, you should shop around and find someone whose work you like, who understands your industry and who has a good reputation. Also, if you find someone who listens to your needs, chances are you will be pleased with your results.

Red Hot Tip!

Free Websites:

There are a lot of ways to create free websites these days. You may choose to get one of these free sites, but keep in mind that if you don't own it, it's not yours. It can get taken down for material the host company deems to be offensive or controversial, or if they go out of business. But the biggest problem is that free websites can't be optimized or ranked. So if you're looking for online exposure, free has a price.

Find a Good Designer

In my line of work, I usually refer out website designers but sometimes a client will ask their nephew or son to design it for them. This is fine if your relatives are actual designers, but most of the time they have simply bootlegged a copy of Dreamweaver and tinkered with it just enough to make them dangerous. They probably won't start blowing up small countries by hitting the wrong button in Dreamweaver, but a poorly-designed site could cost a ton of sales.

Find out the answers to these questions from any potential designer:

- Does your designer know your market/industry?
- Do they provide references?

- Are your designer and programmer the same person? (They shouldn't be!)
- What is their turn-around time?
- Do they meet deadlines? (You might want to search out some of their clients and ask them.)
- How much do they charge for web maintenance?
- Will you own all the rights to your site's design and function?
- Will they provide you with a disc of your design and web files?
- Do you like their work? Ask for samples.
- Are they easy to communicate with?
- Do you get one designer assigned to you or are you working with a team?
- Do they listen to your needs?
- Are they using industry standard programs to build your site?
- Will they provide you with design comps from which to choose?

Domain Name

"Your domain name is not only your address on the Internet, but also your best asset," says Susan Gilbert, CEO of Online Promotion Success. As with the website itself, it's important to understand how your domain name can bolster the success of your branding and marketing strategies.

Susan Gilbert has successfully developed hundreds of websites for herself and her clients, including amarketingexpert.com. Gilbert says that when people launch a website, they often forget the importance of branding with their domain name.

In the physical world, you can distinguish a business because of its structure, window displays or signs. You can tell that a bank is a bank, or a clothing store is indeed a clothing store. Catalogs and brochures also establish the product line: a Fingerhut catalog can tell you that they are fashion retailers.

On the Internet, however, it is an entirely different story. Your domain name is the only clue to your online business. You do not have visual clues: no location, no outside indicators and no store design. Instead, they have to type in a word or a set of words to reach your site. Your prospective visitors have no way of knowing what your site is all about until they find it and read its contents. Who can ever tell that Amazon sells books? Or that Yelp is a search engine? Unlike in the real world where a person can stand on a corner and know instantly that the business in front is a watch store, a record store is at the right corner, and that a restaurant is located down the street. With no physical clues to offer, you only have your domain name to make your business distinguishable from all the rest.

Common Name vs. Proper Name

The need to provide immediate clues to an online business led to the prevalence of generic domain names. Generic names instantly provide the user with an idea of what to expect and look for in a site. eToys.com is a toy store. Women.com caters to women. MyFamily.com is about families, while SmallBusiness.com is for small businesses.

The lure of the generic has been so powerful that some companies pay absurdly high prices to get the name they want. Remember Business.com? A Los Angeles company paid $7.5 million to get the rights to that name. The domains Loans.com and Wines.com were both bought for $3 million. Telephone.com was acquired for $1.75 million, while Bingo.com sold for $1.1 million.

Thus, we see sites (and lots of them!) use generic domain names, and all their possible iterations. Take a site on business planning. We have:

BusinessPlan.com
BusinessPlans.com
Bplans.com
Bizplan.com

And these are just dot-coms. The list does not include all the dot-nets, dot-orgs and other domain wannabes.

But is it working? The problem with generic names is...well, they're generic! While such common names could lead users to your site, they hardly create the zing or magic that makes successful brands. Branding has always been about proper names: McDonald's did not name their store Hamburger. Hertz is not called Car Rental. FedEx is not Mail Carrier. Kodak is not Photographs. Microsoft is not Computer Software.

The right domain name can solidify your business identity, permanently embed it in a user's psyche and garner more attention than a 30 second spot in the Super Bowl. For better branding results, your domain name should be memorable and easy to remember.

Here are seven points Susan offers on how to choose an effective domain name:

1. The shorter the better. Since users will have to type in the domain name, it should be both short and easy to spell. Long generic names, in particular, can be confusing and hard to remember. The consulting firm PriceWaterhouseCoopers' ebusinessisbusiness.com was both complicated and long—and is no longer in use. Thus, it is not hard to imagine why the sixty-five character domain names never caught on. Who could remember (much less have the patience to type correctly) names like learnthemarketingsecretsintheworld.com? Long names are simply too cumbersome.

2. It should be simple to increase recall. Not all short domain names are simple. Some domains combine numbers with letters, resulting in hard-to-remember names like Click2Asia.com and Opus360.com. Combining names and numbers makes it much more difficult to recall and these domains usually make poor brand names.

3. Without keyword stuffing, it can very clearly say what you do. In the city of Issaquah, Washington, issaquahmassagetherapist.com is easy to remember and ranks well for the location and business category.

4. It should be unique and memorable. Remember, you and your business will be reflected in the domain name.

5. It should be easy to say. Word of mouth is a potent communication medium. Tell a few people the domain name and see whether it causes any confusion. If it takes more than two or three seconds for people to get it, you may want to pick something else.

6. It should be personalized. If the situation allows it, you can name your site after yourself. Using a personal name for a domain enhances the publicity potential of your site. "My gift book titled *The Land of I Can* does have its own site," says Susan. "But people really purchase as they get to know more about me. So, getting your name [like www.susangilbert.com] is great for self-promotion."

7. Make sure the website itself reflects your domain name. Don't have a domain name like trendyhandbags.com and then show shoes for sale when the visitor arrives. A domain name must have a message match to your website.

While it may be hard for a domain name to embody all the seven qualities above, choosing a name with these tips in mind will help you develop an Internet brand that will lead to your online success. Remember, it all starts with the brand name, says Gilbert.

Be Your Own Spy

When was the last time you monitored your competitors' websites, or even took a few minutes to look them over? If you don't, maybe you should. Get to know who else is out there sharing your "pond." See what's on their website and what promotions they are running. Doing a periodic competitor check is a healthy way to stay in touch with other people in your industry and get to know the competition. Plus, you can get some great ideas on what needs to be on your website.

HOW TO CREATE THE PERFECT WEBSITE

"Almost overnight, the Internet's gone from a technical wonder to a business must."
— Bill Schrader

Do you remember that old game, Operation? I loved playing it as a kid. When I started I always kept touching the sides of the openings before I could pull out the patient's organs. It never failed, that darned buzzer would go off and I'd have to start again. I played and played and played that game until I could pull out the guy's brain in my sleep. So listen, if you ever have to have surgery of *any* kind, I would like to perform it for you. I mean, I'm an ace at this stuff, right? I can pull plastic kidneys and hearts out of a smiling plastic victim with little or no buzzer anymore!

I'm betting money that despite my talent at Operation, you'd never let me operate on you. You'd at least want to hire someone with a degree—maybe even someone with some experience, rather than a new doc, fresh out of medical school.

While website design might be a long way off from brain surgery, if you're sinking any money at all into a marketing campaign with a site that looks... well, like it needs surgery, then you might be losing money—the kind of money that could feed future marketing efforts. There's also the consideration of the designers that offer a lot for very little money. This may seem like a great idea at the onset, but dig a little deeper and you might find that for all the money you paid (even if the price was great), got you a website that doesn't do what you need it to. If that's the case, your money was wasted.

If I sound preachy, it's for a reason: I used to design my own websites. Yes, I confess. I am guilty of this. I thought, "I don't need no stinkin' designer." But I learned and I learned the hard way. I had a site that wasn't converting because it looked like a dog had designed it after a three-day tequila bender. Some days I look at old web shots of it and wonder "What was I thinking?" Thankfully it's gone, burned to the ground and rebuilt in a site that can stand the test of effectiveness and conversion. It only took me four years to get there.

Yes, site design is a process. I'm not saying that you need to spend four years tinkering with your site—this section alone will save you at least three years and ten months—but you do need to hire the right people. This means more than just people who put together beautiful sites, because beautiful sites don't necessarily convert. I'm not saying that your site needs to be ugly, just that there's a difference between effectiveness and attractiveness.

In this chapter we're going to cover that difference, as well as all the pieces you need to put together a site that's exactly what you need—no more, no less. In fact, we'll even determine what you need with our handy-dandy questionnaire. The only thing you'll need to do is hire the right person to build it, and we'll help you with that, too, with our list of questions to ask before hiring a designer. So now sit back and grab that highlighter. We're ready to send you off on the super highway of website success!

Building Billboards

Between Los Angeles and Las Vegas there's a stretch of I-15 that's just barren desert with you, sand, a cactus or two, a few vultures hoping to get lucky and endless billboards. You're anxious to hit the blackjack tables, so you speed down this stretch of highway as fast as you can, passing billboards at maybe eighty-five miles an hour. Most of the billboards you see will be fairly simple and easy to read. Like this one:

Now that was easy, right? Fairly straightforward, not too much to read. If you passed a billboard that looked like this:

You'd probably ram your car into the billboard and make some vulture very, very happy.

Think of Your Site as a Billboard

If you think of your website as a billboard instead of a website, you'll be much further along than most people. Why? Because at the rate people surf these days, you might as well be speeding to Vegas. Studies have shown that the average surfer used to spend seven seconds on a website before deciding whether or not to click off. Now it's one-fiftieth of a second. That means that you have only a snippet of time to set the hook and prove to your visitors that your site is worthy of their visit.

As surfers we don't read, we scan, and the further we get down the road, the more we're finding that web copy (the text on your website) isn't about writing; it's about writing less. We don't want to think, we just want to click, and preferably we want to be told what to do. A well-designed site is not just one that's light on copy; it's also uncomplicated and very obvious. Have you ever heard of the seventh grade education rule? Well, on the 'Net it's about a fourth grade education level. If you aim lower, you'll hit much higher in your conversion. Now, I'm not saying that surfers are stupid, not even close. In fact, surfers know what they want and won't be fooled or lured into something they're unsure of. The key to remember is that web surfers aren't short on smarts, they're short on time, hence the shrinking window of opportunity to catch someone's attention on the 'Net.

When we're getting a site designed, we have a tendency to want to push everything onto our home page. We cram it full of every piece of everything we've ever done, from writing a book to the time our Little League team took first prize at nationals. Just like that billboard crammed with stuff, we want to fill every inch of our home page with words and pictures and all the kinds of things that will send surfers scrambling for the exit button. I call it surf shock when you land on a site that seems to scream at you from your monitor. These kinds of sites you can't wait to leave.

Avoiding Surf Shock

There are some key ways to avoid surf shock. The first and most obvious is to keep your copy minimal. The next might be selecting the colors. If you have a product and an audience that resonates with yellow, then you might want to have enough yellow on your site to "speak" to them without overwhelming them with a yellow fireball of a site. The colors need to resonate with the audience, not offend them. Pick the wrong colors and you'll end up sending visitors into surf shock.

Listed below are a few characteristics of color that should always be considered when designing your graphics:

- The colors on your site will affect your emotions within 90 seconds of viewing them.

- Colors can motivate or deter your viewer from buying your product. They can also impress and persuade.

- Colors not only intensify the item, they can greatly influence our behavior.

- If you're selling internationally, remember that the effects of color vary among cultures.

- Color choices can send subliminal messages to your viewers. What is your site saying about you?

- Color sends a specific message to your viewers. That said, here are a few color "translations"—find out what your site is *really* saying:

    - White – Stands for truthfulness, purity, cleanliness, devotion and modernity. White is best for a background color on the web, especially for businesses.

    - Red – This is an aggressive color, so use it judiciously. Red suggests strength, sex, excitement, passion, speed and danger. Red is the most emotionally intense color, and did you know it stimulates rapid heartbeat and breathing?

    - Green – An abundant color for sure, and according to industry experts, green is the easiest color on the eye. Green stands for health, fertility, freedom, nature and growth. In business it suggests status and wealth.

- Brown – Hints of kindness, effectiveness, wealth and helpfulness.

  - Black – a classic color, infers elegance, boldness, power, authority, seduction, evil, sophistication and classic. I don't recommend having an entire background in black, it's too hard on the eye, but it's ideal for text on a white or light background.

  - Blue – This is by far the most popular color for websites, especially in business where it suggests fiscal responsibility, security, trust, reliability and dignity.

  - Gray – Lends itself to a more serious tone, suggesting authority, earnestness and practicality. It's also a very traditional color, good for businesses that are more conservative in nature.

  - Pink – A fun color to be sure, and great for those fun, funky female sites. Pink suggests softness, sweetness, femininity, well-being, innocence and nurturing. Hot pink or variants of thereof suggest fun, à la *Sex and the City*.

  - Purple – The royal color infers spirituality, dignity, luxury, wealth, authority and sophistication. It's upscale for businesses and favored by those in artistic professions.

  - Orange – While I'd rarely recommend orange as a website's main color, smears or highlights of it can be effective. Orange suggests playfulness, pleasure, cheer and vibrancy, as well as strength, endurance and ambition.

  - Yellow – Much like orange, you'll want to be cautious using this color. Lots of it can be very hard on the eye, as it's the most difficult color for the eye to process. But used in moderation, yellows hints of sunshine, warmth, cheer and happiness. In business it is appealing to intellectual types and is good for accents. Yellow also enhances concentration and increases metabolism.

Paralysis by Analysis

Does your site resemble Starbucks? A million buttons and links with endless choices for the user? Is it intricate and complicated? Ok, I confess. I'm one of those Starbucks patrons who orders a complicated drink. I don't know how my "black coffee" turned into something that takes three minutes to order, but it does. Most of us are used to Starbucks by now, their complex options and effectively unlimited choices of coffee and non-coffee beverages. Starbucks is trendy and fun, but what if you weren't used to that? What if you were from the moon and you happened into a Starbucks for the first time? Would you be overwhelmed? Probably. When my mother visits from Belgium, we invariably end up in a Starbucks. She'll stare at the menu for about ten minutes and then give up and just get a black coffee.

Unfortunately, while it works well for Starbucks, it won't work for your site. Giving your user too many options turns into "analysis paralysis," and they'll click off faster than you can say, "double tall, non-fat, no-foam latte." Your site must be clean, simple and easy for the user to find what they are seeking.

Red Hot Tip!

Whatever you do and whatever your business is, your home page should have only one goal. Whether that's selling a product, selling a service or selling you, you need to pick one overarching objective for the home page.

What's your goal? What do you want people to do when they land on your site?

How People Surf

Numerous studies have been performed about how people surf. As we discussed above, people scan text. They don't read every word, but look for the most important pieces that will directly benefit them. Remember that it's all about the WIIFM factor (what's in it for me?). The first question your visitors will ask themselves is, "Why am I here?" or (even worse) "Why am I here and not somewhere else?" That's why it's key for your site to address all of these issues. More importantly, your home page must address all of these questions and give people a reason to stay.

Before we get there you'll need to understand how the eye works once it lands on a site. Here's a screenshot image of our home page (www.amarketingexpert.com)—the circles on the site clearly show how the eye moves through the surfing experience. You might be surprised at what you learn from this experience:

Now let's take a look at the site without the circles so you can get an idea of how we decided to push in our information, and what information we chose to present.

#1: This is the most important piece of the home page. The primary goal of your home page should be reflected here. If you want to sell a product, get newsletter sign-ups or any other important activity, this will be a key spot. Why? Because we read from left to right, so when someone lands on your site, they scan landing on the right side first.

#2: Once the eye scans #1, it heads right over to the #2 spot with one question in mind: WIIFM? So #2 and 3 must answer that question for them. As you're writing your site copy, remember to think *newspaper* copy. When you read a newspaper (if you still do), you know that the headline is the most important part. The article then leads with the most important information and the importance descends in a hierarchal fashion throughout the piece. The same holds true for these pieces of your site. We chose a tag line that indicates that while our book promotion is powerful, it's not going to be too taxing on the buyer. We followed that with some short and snappy copy—notice from the copy that it states not only the benefits, but uses a lot of "you" language. AME found in extensive research that when visitors land on this page, it is not about the company or the products we have, it's about them and how we can help them navigate the maze of marketing and publicity options. And did you happen to notice all the calls to action we have on the page: *Find out More*, *Call Now*, *Download our Catalog*? It's important to tell people what you want them to do. Finally, bear in mind that social proof is powerful, which is why we have the row of books at the top of the page and the reference to bestsellers in the copy. Look at our actual copy in this page:

There isn't a lot there, right? But the call to action "find out more" is prominent. Susan Gilbert encouraged us to have lots of ways for folks to get information because that's the primary goal of the home page. She also advised us that visitors need to be told what to do; if you make them guess, they will leave your site. Give them action steps: *Find out More* and *Buy Now!*

Things to Avoid

Susan offers additional website advice: "Avoid building a Flash website." Flash sites are made up of images which can be viewed by a visitor but are not searchable by search engines like Google. Yes, you can build a whole second website that is seen 'behind the scenes' by search engines—but it's not the best solution. Your site should be made of searchable text and lots of it. The more relevant content you have, the more likely your site will appear in a SERP (search engine results page). Also, Flash sites take longer to load, and while we would like to think that our viewers have the patience to wait, the reality is that they will probably move on to another site.

The WordPress and Joomla! platforms are great content building options that are also easily editable by you without requiring a programmer or technician to make changes and updates. In fact, WordPress is in use by 48% of the top 100 blogs in the world. This is an increase from the 32% from three years ago and includes Mashable, TechCrunch, Boing Boing and the Bits blog from *The New York Times* to name just a few, Susan notes.

Website Must-Dos

- ✓ Optimize your pictures. Web images should be no more than 72 dpi.
- ✓ Be consistent with your navigation. If your readers get confused, they are less likely to buy your product.
- ✓ Create powerful title tags for each page of your site. Each tag should be no more than 66 characters long, including spaces. It should include relevant keywords and search terms. Lastly, Susan points out that the title tag is what people will see on a SERP, so it needs to appeal to your audience as well.

Where to Put Your Buy Button

Once you build your site and everything is working, do not make your visitor search all over your site in order to buy from you! Put your BUY NOW button in an obvious, easy-to-find space. You may be laughing now, but we've worked with many businesses who buried the BUY NOW button so deep in the site, it was impossible to find!

Capture Them

One of the best things you can do for your site is add a means to capture a name and email address so you can market to your visitors again and again and again. At AME we have a newsletter that goes out bi-weekly. It's packed full of marketing ideas, tips and hints for authors, businesses, speakers and publishers. While the newsletter may require a lot of time to write and create, it's worth its weight in gold because it allows us to stay on the radar screen of our customers and web visitors. "Marketing wisdom," says Susan Gilbert "shows us that your best customer is your current customer. That means if someone is interested enough to visit your site, they're probably interested enough to learn more about your current products and your future products. How do you notify them? By capturing their email addresses."

Maybes Rule

When it comes to the Internet, "maybes" rule. Unlike storefront businesses, you don't have to get a "yes" or "no" answer. You can get a "maybe" and still make the sale:

- "Maybe I'll sign up for the newsletter now and decide if I want the product later," or

- "Maybe I'll just get one of the reports and come back later for the service."

Maybes keep you in the game and give you a chance to sell something later on.

Never Use a Squeeze Page as Your Main Website

Squeeze pages are designed to "squeeze" your email address out of you by offering you fabulous (free) incentives or opportunities to buy. When done correctly, squeeze pages can be a great way to grow your list, but unfortunately many folks use these as standalone websites. This is a huge mistake. Squeeze pages are fine if they're a page within your site, but when they're a site unto themselves, it becomes tricky. Why? Well, the squeeze page is designed to block consumers from getting to content unless they give you their email address. The same is true for search engines, too, since they can't fill out the forms to spider your site. This means that they can't spider your site either, since they can't get to all of your fabulous content. Second, journalists are not going to give up their email address to get to your media room. So if a press person lands on your site and finds nothing but a squeeze page, you've now also lost a media interview.

Pop-ups Work

Everyone says they hate pop-ups, but statistically they've been proven to be effective. Pop-ups are particularly good for (1) getting mailing list sign-ups; (2) giving away a free report; and (3) offering a special on the page visitors are about to leave (such as your "thank you for subscribing" page). You want to create a visually interesting pop-up that offers something for free. If people are willing to give you their name and email, you need to be willing to give them something of value too.

Link to Other Sites

If you're going to go through all the trouble of putting yourself "out there" on the Internet, you should make sure the footprint you leave is lasting. You can do this by developing a list of sites your consumer will find valuable, as well as sites that have a long-standing and solid reputation in the Internet community. My father used to say, "If you lie down with dogs, you'll get fleas." The same can be said for the sites you partner with. Don't just accept links to your sites willy-nilly, partner with sites that are a reflection of your own message. Once you have this list, remember that relationships take time. Don't expect to get top billing on the first go around—you may have to work hard to contribute to the site or offer other content or freebies to the site's visitors. We'll look more at link building in a minute.

Contact Information

Don't forget to list your contact information on the home page. This step is often overlooked. Make sure your contact info is easy to find; don't hide the contact email or phone number. If you make people hunt for this, I promise you they won't invest the time to find it

TURNING YOUR WEBSITE INTO A SELLING MACHINE!

"If Al Gore invented the Internet, I invented spell check."
— Dan Quayle

If you're ready to get more traffic to your site (and who isn't?), just throwing up a website won't cut it. Here's a quick guide for getting more quality visitors.

Finding Your Keywords

First, figure out what you want your keywords to be. What sort of searches do you want to come up for? This is important because pinning yourself to the wrong search term, could get you poor results. Getting someone too early or too late in the buying process may get you a lot of traffic, but it may not be the right kind. Figure out where their point of entry is. This isn't something that you can search online using Google AdWords, Trends or Insight—it's something you learn by researching your market. I learned about this when I did my own research. I plugged in a bunch of keywords I wanted to rank for to see what came up.

First, gather some search terms. Not all of these will be your keywords, they are just your starting point. They might end up being perfect or you might scrap the list and start over. Your research will point you in the right direction.

Let's say you have a series of keywords you are considering but you aren't sure what other variables folks might be searching on. Hop on over to Soovle.

com. When you land on this site, you'll see a simple box to plug in your keyword. When you do, you'll get back variations of searches that come up in sites like YouTube, Google, Yahoo! and Bing. It will also show these terms as used on Amazon.com, which can be helpful if you are selecting tags to go with your business. You'll want to spend some time here, clicking the various links to find different ways that consumers search on these keywords. You also might find a better search term than what you currently use, or it might validate your research. Either way, it's a fantastic site and one I use often.

Once you get your keywords nailed down, Google AdWords is a great place to research their popularity. You want to know that your keywords are getting enough searches to matter to your traffic. If you go to Google AdWords, punch in your keywords and then turn off the broad match so you narrow down your results a bit more. You can also play around with "exact" and "phrase," but I usually stick with all three of those unchecked to see what kind of results I get. Generally I look for Global Monthly Searches that are above 650; I'd rather it be higher, but if you are searching a niche term, that might be the best you can do.

How to Use Keywords

You now need to know how to use the keywords you spent so much time finding. First and foremost, incorporate them into the copy on your home page. I recommend keeping the verbiage on your home page to no more than 250 words, but make sure that this text is keyword rich. Address your visitors' concerns, not yours. Remember that the first few lines of your website copy will show up in searches, so make sure it's relevant to the audience.

The URL you're using could make a difference. When we did our keywords, we established that we wanted to come up for the term "Book marketing," so we started using it everywhere, in our Facebook Page (http://www.facebook.com/bookmarketingame), on our YouTube Channel (http://www.youtube.com/user/BookmarketingAME) and even in our URL. I bought bookmarketingAME.com. Now, we don't use this URL per se, it just points to our main domain name which is amarketingexpert.com. Why did we do that? Because the use of your core search terms is key to driving traffic and getting higher in the search rank. Want proof? Before we did all of this, our website was generally at the bottom of page one on Google or on page two when you plugged in "book marketing" in the search bar. Three months after we made these changes (keywords on the home page and keywords in our Facebook branding, YouTube and URL), we came up #3 in search, sometimes #2 and on a stupendously good day, we're #1. Now that's a great traffic jam!

You also can and should use keywords in your blog posts. Not so much that your posts don't make sense (this is called keyword stuffing), but sprinkle them throughout your content, like we did with this chapter (using words like marketing, book marketing, keywords, etc.).

You should also use the keywords in your YouTube videos and in Alt tags in pictures on your website. Keywords are fantastic, and once you go through the work of finding them, you can use them over and over again.

Watch Your Traffic

Get Google Analytics to help you monitor your website traffic—any SEO expert will tell you that's about the best analytics software you can use. Once you insert this bit of code into your site, you'll be able to determine what kind of traffic you're getting and from where. How are people finding you (i.e. what keywords are they using to get to your site), and what sites are pulling in your traffic? Very helpful information. You should plan to check your traffic monthly, if not more often.

Additional Tips for Driving Traffic

There's a fun little site you've probably already heard of called Google Trends. It will show you trending topics, and you can also plug in your keywords to find trends in your area of expertise. But here's the real fun part. I try to watch Google Trends every so often, maybe once or twice a week if I'm really stumped on what to blog on. Under "Hot Searches" you'll find the top items that consumers are searching on. If you can write a blog post on these topics or make any of them relevant to your message, you can surge traffic on your site. Keep in mind that your topic must be relevant! Everyone has become careful about authenticity of content since the Google Panda Update (http://www.seomoz.org/blog/beat-google-panda).

Another great site is Google Insights. This will show you areas (worldwide) that may have a potential interest in your topic and the locations that get the most searches. If you're looking to dig into particular markets, you can really get a sense of where the interest lies, and you might even be surprised. When

I searched on book marketing, I found some of the highest searches in India. You can also see how searches rank for your particular topic and how they have trended over time. I find this very interesting when I'm researching a business or book topic for marketing or a particular angle for a pitch we're considering.

Conclusion

Keywords don't have to be these mysterious search terms that only your website or SEO person knows about. Finding and using the right keywords can make a big difference to any website and, especially, to your sales. Also, even though we talked about thousands of hits on a site, you don't really need that many to make a difference to your bottom line. Good, quality traffic and a solid site that's converting is all it takes to reap your own online rewards!

What The Heck Is ALT Text?

Says Susan Gilbert, "While you can 'see' a graphic or photo online, the search engine bots cannot. Alt text provides a search engine with a 'translation' of the content of the image (a search engine can't read the text in an image—at least not yet). Additionally, using the alt tag gives Google (or Bing, etc) that extra little bit of information about your photo to give it more importance for your keywords. Go to one of your favorite sites and mouse over an image. You'll probably see text appear; this is an Alt tag. Alt text is presented in place of an image if the link to the image is broken or the visitor is using a text-only browser. Including Alt text in your web pages is a good design practice."

Red Hot Tip!

Google Fight (www.googlefight.com) is not affiliated with Google but it's a helpful site when trying to determine a good keyword or keyword phrase. Plug the words into Google Fight and let them "fight" over which is more popular in a Google search.

WORDS ON YOUR WEBSITE

"While modern technology has given people powerful new communication tools, it apparently can do nothing to alter the fact that many people have nothing useful to say."
— Leo Gomes

Define Your Goals

Before you put pen to paper to write your sales copy for your website, be clear about your goals. We talked earlier about your goals for building a website—pull those out and look at them again. While you may be building the website to sell more cookies, as you start to look at the broader reach of your message, your goals might change. Perhaps you can put together gift baskets too. Make sure the copy you are about to write targets those goals. And don't forget to use all the keywords you just selected!

Sell the Benefits

Save the small talk for your next cocktail party. When it comes to filling websites with words, beginners tend to lean towards what I like to call the "cocktail party approach to website copy." What do I mean by this? Well, let's pretend you're at a cocktail party, you're huddled with a group of friends gabbing about everything under the sun, and around you hundreds of other conversations are mingling with your own, making the voices sound like a hum. That's what it's like to a website visitor when you cram a lot of cocktail party copy onto your home page. It's confusing and it's white noise. Chances are good that it will result in a "click" signaling the party's end, your visitor long gone.

Instead, write copy that speaks to your readers and tells them the benefits of your product. Sell the sizzle not the steak.

Make it Scannable

Remember that Internet users scan websites and that relates to how you write good copy. When I spoke to Susan Gilbert, she told me about the elements of good copy. "The Internet has made 'brochure-style' writing obsolete. Studies have clearly shown that people do not read websites—they skim them. That means your copy must be written to be eye catching, visually compelling and keep the visitor on your site."

How do you write scannable website copy? By incorporating lots of

- white space
- bullet points
- highlighted and **bolded** words
- images

In addition, your copy needs to use simple words, short sentences and include the keywords your site visitor probably used to find your site in a search engine.

Stay On Point

You should distill your web copy down to the most important points and eliminate everything else. You have less than a second to grab someone's attention. Don't risk overwhelming your reader. Remember, it's not about you, it's about them.

Use Captivating Headlines

Be sure to make your message obvious. Use headlines, lists and bold text to convey your message. Spend some serious time really thinking about a catchy headline.

What Do I Get Out of the Deal?

When it comes to sales copy, the WIIFM (what's in it for me) factor is more important than ever. I have already mentioned the importance of selling the benefits when writing good copy. Then I talked with Susan Gilbert and she emphasized this point: "People want to know what benefit they'll receive from buying your product or service. Don't be shy—tell them! Will they get free delivery? Will they make more money? Will they look better? Although visitors may want to know you, the person, sales copy is much more about telling them how their life will be better, safer, happier and richer once they've bought from you." Hopefully between Susan and me we have hammered this point home.

Too Much Is Too Much

One of my personal pet peeves is websites that give me every piece of instruction under the sun. I don't care if I'm developing cold fusion, if you give me more than 300 words of directives—I'm out. Keep it simple and stick to the point.

Don't Yell

Another pet peeve is people who yell at me. That's my mother's job. When you use lots of CAPS OR EXCLAMATION POINTS (!!!!!!!!!!!!), it seems like you're yelling. Let's be honest, no one can be *that* excited about anything.

Bullet Points

As I have said several times, people will scan a page for interesting tidbits of information before they read it. Creating a bullet point list makes it easy for the reader to see the points you are making and get more interested in what you are selling. Most top viewed websites have at least one set of bullet points.

"Read More" Buttons

If you have a lot to say, try summarizing it into a succinct paragraph and then link it with a Read More button to the rest of the article on a landing page deeper in your site. These buttons keep your site free of over-clutter and long articles.

Consider a Professional

The reality, of course, is that most folks, including authors, don't really like writing sales copy. And that's okay. However, unless the world is filled with your relatives, you're going to need sales copy to sell your product, service or book. So if you feel you don't have the skill or desire to write good sales copy, hire a professional to write the words that will help you strike website copy gold.

Margins

Bring in your margins. No one wants to read all the way across the screen, so to combat that we bring in our margins to keep them reading and maintain their attention span. Also, don't overwhelm them with a page that's bigger than their monitor. Make it easy on the reader.

Narrow Columns

Avoid running the text all the way across the screen. Break it up into short, succinct, easily digestible, narrow columns. This advice is based on the same premise as bringing in your margins. Narrow columns are easier to read and less likely to fatigue your reader.

Blurbs

When it comes to underlined text in a blurb or excerpt, experts suggest limiting these as well, as they are perceived as visual "breaks" and stop the reader's momentum. And speaking of blurbs, researchers have found that the "hot spot" on any blurb, paragraph or header is the left side, meaning that the first few words are the most significant to any text. In fact, attention spans are so short that surfers often only stay focused on a line of text, blurb or headline for less than a second.

Use Links

An obvious benefit of web writing is that you have an opportunity to link to other important areas on your site. Here you can reference resources, news sources, audio clips, other relevant websites and your own calls to action.

Use Relevant Keywords

Try to use words that are relevant to the content within your site or article. Words that other people might type into a search engine looking for the information you offer are your target keywords. The more you can do to help people find you, the better.

Copyright

Remember to copyright your material and keep it current. Protect yourself by placing the year of the content's creation and a © at the bottom of each webpage.

Picking the Perfect Font

Size Does Matter

When it comes to font sizes, many people think that the larger the font, the more likely a surfer is to stay. Make the font too small, and you'll drive people off of your site, right? Wrong. Studies have shown that to a point, a smaller size discourages scanning and encourages a more focused viewing experience. The same goes for headlines. When headlines on a page are too big, surfers launch into scan mode, quickly skimming the page for something to grab and keep their attention.

Picking the Perfect Font

When it comes to a font for your website, it's easy to get carried away. Temptation might dictate that you use a fancy scroll or a really bold font. Wrong. The challenge with using unique fonts is that the person at the other end might not be able to read it. When you land on a site that's full of that horrible Courier font (my apologies to all you Courier lovers out there, this usually indicates that the site is using a font your computer can't read.

Sometimes, when people want to use special fonts, they'll turn them into graphics instead. But that's good and bad. First, search engines can't spider graphics (we'll discuss the spider factor later). And second, it increases the load time of your website. The trick really is to pick a font (preferably a sans serif) that's both readable and friendly to the eye, meaning that it doesn't tire the eye the way a serif font does. So, what's the difference between the two? When a web designer talks about a serif typeface, he means fonts like Times or Century Schoolbook, where the characters (letters) have little accents or curves. For example, look at a capital "T" in the Times font. The small downward curves that appear at each end of the cross on the top and the inverted curves at the foot of the letter are known as serifs. "Sans" is French and literally means "without." Now look at a capital "T" in Helvetica or Arial. The character doesn't have those little accents, thus indicating it is a Sans Serif typeface.

Example:	Times New Roman	T
	Arial	T

Don't Get Font-Happy

Do not overwhelm your site with a bunch of different fonts. It simply takes too much work for the reader to process the different letters and fonts. Nothing will send your visitors away faster.

YOUR ROCKIN' RED HOT MEDIA ROOM

"Don't say anything online that you wouldn't want plastered on a billboard with your face on it."
— Erin Bury

Did you know that second only to your blog, the media room should be the most updated page on your website? When was the last time you updated your media room? For most of us, it's probably been a while. Though most people tend to put up media rooms and then forget about them. But more and more, a good, informative media room should be consistently updated. We've found through research, reading and our own experiences that it's not just the media that visits this page. That's why the term "media room" is a bit misleading. It's actually a great place to inform, entertain and educate your customer on you, your products, your service or message and the things you've been up to. And often it's the first place a prospective buyer will go to for more information on you and your work.

Out with the Old

While printed media kits aren't dead per se, the media (and your customers) generally find that a kit online serves much the same purpose. And if you're doing all the right things in your Internet Publicity campaign, the media will soon find their way to your virtual door. Keep in mind that your media or press room will grow over time. If you're worried that you don't have a lot to include, never fear. The list of things to include in your media room will add up quickly, and soon your press room will be filled with all the things the media loves. They key is to make this page fun, informative and interactive. Give whoever is perusing it a reason to stay for a while, a reason to return and a reason to interview you for their magazine, blog or show.

Media Room Tips

The old way of doing media rooms was to have a list of your press releases and maybe a link or two to media stories about you, and that was that. Now media rooms are almost the nerve center of your entire website. Here's a quick rundown of what should (and shouldn't) be in your media room. Keep in mind that components will vary depending on your topic, brand and focus, so if you can't include all of these, that's ok. Better to have only those components related to your product than ones that don't make any sense at all.

- *Downloadable pictures* – Make sure these are in 300 dpi and 72 dpi.

- *Bio / About You section* – People want to know who you are, so tell them! This is especially helpful if a media person is trying to gather information for an article and wants some background on you.

- *Press releases with live links* – Live links in a press release are a great way to get traffic back to your site, but guess what? It works well in reverse, too. News posted to your site gets spidered very quickly, so including links and keywords will greatly enhance the visibility of both the media room and your press release. In fact, another quick tip is this: instead of placing ads, issue a (well-written and optimized) press release. No kidding. Press releases are far better than ads on the Internet. You'll get spidered, you'll get ranking, and best of all, you'll get traffic to your site.

- *New product / service information* – This is the perfect place for sharing past, current and future information on your product/service. Be boastful! This is your chance!

- *Tip sheets* – We all know the media loves tip sheets, but guess what: your customers do, too. Fill your press room with any you've created.

- *Where you've been featured* – Be very generous with this. Don't assume that if you have only been featured online that you should not list that. List everything! The more you can populate this room with links that make you look like the busy person you are, the more attractive you'll be to your buyer and to the media.

- *Ideas for stories* – If a reporter is perusing your site looking for story ideas, why not give it to him? Creating a pop-up box that says "Here's how (insert your name) can help you with your story" is a great way to generate ideas for the media and get yourself a mention in an upcoming story.

- *Bragging rights* – If you have testimonials or reviews, place them here too. While it's always good to sprinkle testimonials/reviews throughout your site, this is another great place to list them. Regardless of whether the visitor to your media room is the media or a reader, people like what other people like!

- *Any information on how to buy* – Don't make people hunt for information. The other day I was on a site looking for book pricing. I had to send an email to get a list of pricing. Why? Because it was confidential? Doubtful. But most people don't think to remove the extra steps. Shorten the staircase. Meaning: remove needless steps to the sales close. Put pricing, information sheets, whatever you have up on your media room so folks don't have to go on a hunting expedition for it.

- *Events* – I took events off my website a long time ago. Why? Because I do so much pop-up stuff that I had a hard time keeping up with it. There's nothing worse than an outdated events page, but if you can keep yours up, great! Keep it current. The activity will look great in your media room.

Don't limit yourself to the items mentioned above; experiment with other media room ideas that might not be listed here. Videos, for example, might be another great addition. The key is to start thinking of your media room as a place to present yourself, not just to the media but to the world. This will change how you view this very important page on your site and help turn a ho-hum page into a rockin' red hot media room.

CONVERTING SURFERS INTO CUSTOMERS

The most overlooked advantage to owning a computer is that if they foul up, there's no law against whacking them around a little.
— Eric Porterfield

Imagine this: You go to your local Bloomingdales and find that they shoved all of their products into the basement. Yes, it's true. All of their inventory is in the basement and worse yet, the night janitor locked the basement and left with the key. What would you do? Well, if you're like most people, you'd probably leave. Admittedly, I got this analogy idea from a great quote: "Trying to drive sales to a site that isn't converting is like driving customers to your store and leaving the doors locked; they aren't going to climb through the window." Bryan Eisenberg & Jeffrey Eisenberg, *Call to Action* (Wizard Academy Press)

Your site is not that different from a store. In fact, it *is* a store. Think about the last time you were in a department store. How did you find your way around? Probably those nifty signs hanging from the ceiling or the placard by the escalator. You were given directions, not just left to fend for yourself. There was also an order to how things were placed in the store. The same is true for your website. In order to drive visitors through your site, you'll need to make sure that your website directs them just like the signs in a department store and that the way the site is divided up makes sense. Figure out what they came to the site for, and then create the signage accordingly.

Ask yourself what is the number one reason people visit your site. If this question seems confusing (and early on in the process it might be), consider this:

In some cases you won't know why people visit your site, in other cases it might be because they're seeing information they need. That's what I would say the number one reason is for visiting websites—people want help. My consumers want help with marketing. See? It's not that hard, but it is a bit of a process. Now you try:

The number one reason people visit my site is:

____

There are (hopefully) going to be more reasons that your consumers visit your site—or there might just be one—but likely you're looking at two or three.

List them here:

____

____

____

____

____

These reasons you've listed should all be represented on your home page. Make sure you address your visitors' needs, give them what they want and make it obvious to them where to click to get there. Remember, visitors don't want to just "click here," they want to fix something, buy something or find a solution to a problem they're having. Good conversion is never about you, it's always about the visitor.

So what's a good percentage of conversion? Surprisingly, a 2% conversion rate is pretty standard. What that means is that if only 2% of your visitors do something, you're doing well. By "do something" I mean take any action that helps your business: sign up for your newsletter or blog or perhaps make a purchase.

Although conversion relies heavily on good sales copy, it's also about doing everything you can to get a site visitor from Point A (your home page) through the funnel to Point B (buying something).

Factors impacting conversion include:

- making your site easy to navigate
- giving a guarantee
- ensuring a safe ordering process
- giving customers access to you
- social proof (potential buyers like to know that other people have bought your book and love it).

How Popular Are You?

Who's watching you? Is it a popularity contest? It might be. Check out LinkPopularity.com to see how many search engine links you've got out there and how your site ranks in the grand scheme of things.

The Bottom Line Key to SEO Success

There is one key to success online, and let me tell you now, technology is a piece of it. Yes, the technical side is important and has a very key role to play. Get the technology right without another critical ingredient and failure is guaranteed. What is this secret sauce? People.

"People" are the key to your success, online or off. Let me explain. Take a look at this list and tell me what they all have in common:

- Subscribers
- Traffic

- Links
- Social Media Votes
- Comments
- Search Engine Results
- Advertisers
- Sales

Got it? They all rely on other people! You might think that SEO is all about technical tweaks and tricks. Black arts, keyword stuffing, and getting the right number of keywords in the right places. But I would argue the best Search Engine Optimizers are actually masters of psychology—Social Optimizers if you will. Your best links come from other bloggers. Links and anchor text are key to search results. Social media is partly about phrasing headlines and descriptions, but it is mostly about getting votes. Votes come from people.

Get the people side right and you have won half the battle. Focus on people first; when your audience is happy, you will find the rest a whole lot easier!

HOW TO ANALYZE YOUR WEBSITE TRAFFIC

"The Internet is like a gold-rush; the only people making money are those who sell the pans."
— Will Hobbs

For many of us, traffic and website analytics are very foreign ideas. But understanding traffic and reading website analytics reports doesn't have to be a complicated endeavor. First up, let's break down the terminology:

Page views: Each time someone lands on your site (when they load one of your pages) it generates a page view. Keep in mind that this tallies regardless of who visits or how many times they've been to the site. To some degree it is a bad measurement of traffic. We all love returning visitors, but most of us really care about those valuable first time folks.

Visits: This measure shares how many users have spent time on your website, regardless of the number of pages each user views.

Unique visitors: This is an important stat and as the name implies, this metric counts only the unique users who visit the site. If a particular visitor comes to the site every day, it still only counts as one visit.

Pages/visit: This metric shows you how many pages a visitor perused during each session. The higher this number, the better.

Average visit duration: How much time do users spend on the site during each visit? While you want someone to spend a long time on a site, the average time spent is generally 3-5 min and sometimes less. Obviously longer is better, but currently the only site that gets massive visit duration is Facebook, with an average of twenty minutes per visit.

Bounce rate: This number indicates people who "bounce" off of the page. So, someone visit and then decide they are either in the wrong place or you've sent them into "surf shock" and they leave. Generally the lower the number the better, but the average bounce rate is around 50-59%.

% new visits: This measure is the percentage of your traffic from first-time users who have never been to the site before. If you're eager to get repeat people to your site (and this will often depend on the nature of your business) you'll want this number lower than your repeating visitor number.

Understanding Google Analytics

These days, most websites use Google Analytics, a service I briefly mentioned earlier, to measure traffic. It's considered by most web designers to be the gold standard of measurement, and best of all, it's free.

Getting Google Analytics is easy. You simply register on the site and it will give you a snippet of code that will go on each page of your website. Your web person can add this if it wasn't installed when your site was built. Most hosting companies come with a C-panel backend that measures traffic. Even so, I highly recommend getting Google Analytics for accuracy and some other reasons you'll see in a minute.

Once you set up Google Analytics, give it a few days to gather data. Once you do, you'll start to see numbers appear on your dashboard. Google Analytics continues to update their system and recently launched a beta version of real time traffic, available. Once you're logged in you can find it here:

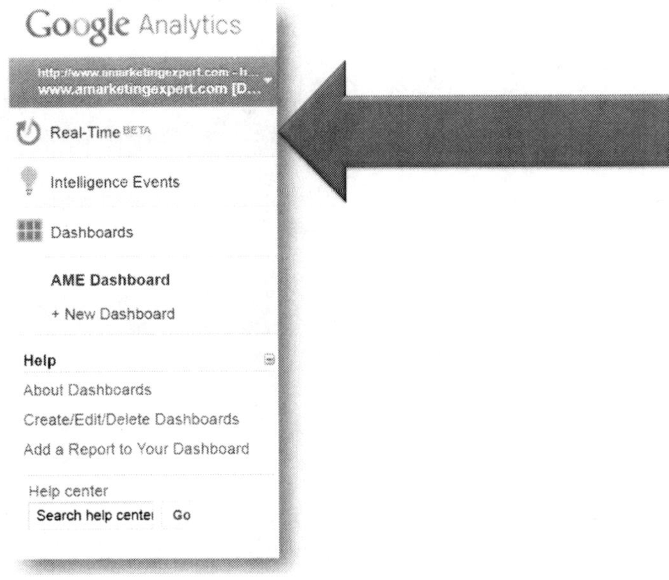

I tend to watch these real-time traffic numbers pretty closely. It's a great tool if you're on top of a promotion, letting you see what kind of traffic you're driving to your website in real time.

Getting to Know Your Data

When you first start looking through the numbers, you'll want to get a sense of the things we described above: Page Views, Bounce Rate, etc. If you're worried that your bounce rate is too high, consult your web person to see if there's anything you can do to lower it. One of the areas I spend a lot of time on is the Traffic from All Sources page, so I can gauge what hits are coming from where. Not only will this help me create referring traffic from various channels, but it also helps me know what's working and what isn't. You can find this area here. Click on Traffic Sources and then All Traffic:

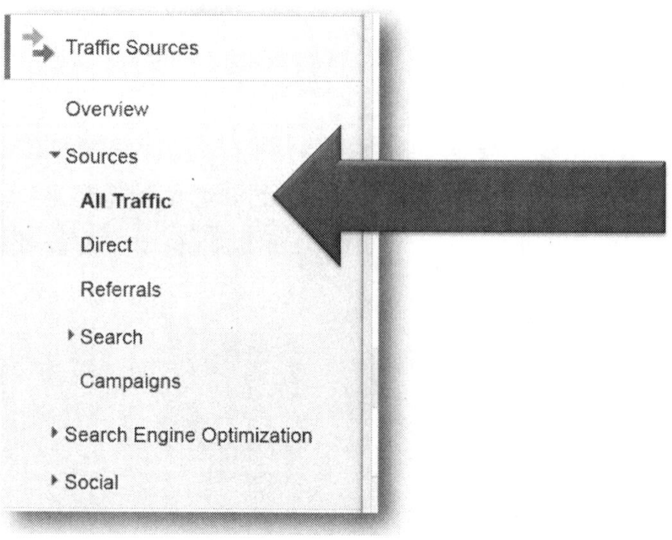

Measuring Social Media

One of the most exciting additions to Google Analytics has been their tracking of social media. This is a fantastic tool that lets you see how much of your traffic is coming from social media. So, what's a good mix? I think half of your traffic should come from social media; the rest should come organically from Google. Here's a snapshot of what these two graphs look like:

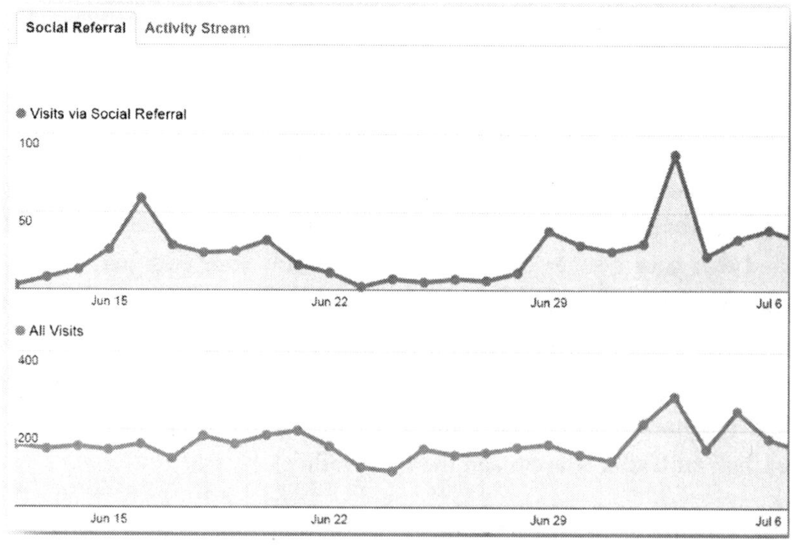

The top bar shows you the social media referrals, with a comparison chart to all traffic, which is super helpful. You don't need to do anything to set this up. Google tracks social traffic automatically.

Measuring AdWords

Google Analytics can also connect to your AdWords campaign, allowing you to measure how your online ads are performing. If you run ads on your site, click *Content > AdSense > Overview* to see which pages are earning the most revenue (and how much). You'll need to link them together in the AdSense tool first.

How much traffic you get and how well it's converting will depend on your reach and your website, but knowing these numbers is important. Remember that the significance of each category will depend largely on the industry you're in. If you want lots of returning visitors, then the percent of new visits number will need to be lower. If you're looking for lots of new traffic then unique visitors is what you need to pay attention to.

Getting to know your traffic is not only important, but mandatory if you're going to know how effective your online marketing is. Also, knowing your Google Analytics numbers will show you if there's a problem on your site, like low conversion, which could be because of a broken page or broken link.

PART THREE:
RED HOT SOCIAL MEDIA

"Never let a computer know you're in a hurry."
— Author Unknown

SOCIAL MEDIA PUBLICITY

"URLs are the 800 numbers of the 1990s."
— Chris Clark

What Exactly Is Social Media?

When I was growing up, I used to watch quaint shows on TV about country living, friendly small towns or deserted islands with castaways. Back then, we didn't have Twitter, Facebook, or Mashable to tell us which shows were hot. We watched and discovered this for ourselves, or we found out at the local grocery store, coffee shop or drycleaners. Word of mouth was spread by people; viewers who enjoyed the shows. Often, I'd try a show based on someone's recommendation. Gossip, of course, spread the same way. In small towns the gossip grapevine spread whatever news needed passing around quickly. Occasionally, written methods of spreading the news like letters or newspapers did the trick. Phones worked the same way, and back when towns had switchboard operators, they usually spread most of the gossip.

As technology improved and phones, cell phones and pagers (remember those?) came into being, we were also introduced to websites and the now dreaded (for some) email. In the early days of website design, it took a lot of programming and sites were very static and unchanging, much like a billboard the world could see. Whatever was on the home page was pretty much all the site offered. There were no blogs and no evolving messages. Email, on the other hand, allowed for a continuous information exchange like the written letter, only much, much faster.

In a very short time, techno whizzes created a way to make websites easily changeable so you and I could manage the content ourselves. The term "user-friendly" became part of people's vocabulary. Then they took the good parts of email—like instant information transmission—and added to that the ability to form groups. This group function turned out to be huge, because a couple with a newborn child could now post information and photos on their social site, knowing all the grandparents and relatives would see it instantly (if they wanted to). And that's what social media really is: It allows you to select people and designate which information they see.

One aspect of this I want to make sure you fully understand is the speed at which this information spread occurs. In the Middle Ages, if something happened in Rome a person would have to share the information by foot, horse or boat. It took up to a year of difficult and dangerous travel to go from Rome to England. If the information needed to be in writing, a scribe wrote it by hand using ink and a goose quill with a sharp point.

Then Gutenberg invented the printing press, and suddenly written information could be duplicated and sent out much faster. Still, the written book had to travel from Rome to England by foot, horse or boat, so the travel time was not really improved. What Gutenberg improved was the *accuracy* of the information, as each copy would be exactly the same. Improving the *speed* would take much longer.

By the mid-1800s not much had changed, when suddenly the telegraph appeared. Using bursts of electricity to send coded signals, the speed of information delivery leapt forward. If something happened in New York City in the morning, some town in California could get news of it within twenty-four hours. (The news had to be retransmitted from station to station.) When the telephone arrived, person-to-person calls increased the speed to about as fast as it would ever get.

Now if you want to tell your father something, you can call, email or text and all are about the same speed. With social media—or social networks as they are also called—you have this same speed at your fingertips. Combining that speed with the ability to reach hundreds (or thousands) of friends instantly and the spread of news, products, restaurants or books is massive. And when your friends hit the button and send it to their group of friends, the information can turn *viral*. That's what social media is: the ability to receive news and spread news quickly to people you know or have some type of relationship with. Think Facebook, Twitter and LinkedIn.

These social networks provide tools that enable members to configure a customized version of a user page, create profiles and bios, manage invites and contact lists, interact with each other via multiple channels and upload photos, video and music files. Interaction tools include built-in instant messaging, chat rooms, bulletin boards, public notes, private messages and comments ("in reply to") on messages. These are but some of the tools available to you to spread the word about your product or service.

Why Does Social Media Work?

Remember being in high school and wanting to hang with the cool kids? Well, maybe you were one of them. If you were, lucky you. But if you are like most of us, you weren't in the popular clique. These days marketing is sort of like being back in high school, but it's a popularity contest that's skewed a bit differently. Marketing, to a large degree, is about *social proof*. What is social proof? It's a sort of social influence where you assume the behavior of others is appropriate given a certain situation. Long waiting lines are a great example. Have you ever observed a long line that spilled out the front door, even winding around the building? You probably wondered what was going on, didn't you? You may even have stood in line with them for a time to find out what all the excitement was about. Social proof is partially driven by numbers. Let's say you're looking at a particular group of organizations, all catering to the same area of expertise. You look at their Facebook Pages and discover that one organization has 50,000 likes, while the others have less than 200. Which page are you most likely to join?

Social proof is also driven by consumer endorsements. People like what other people like, and word can spread about a new car, soft drink or TV show in almost the blink of an eye. Clever marketers can use this to their advantage with tricks such as the velvet rope in front of a club. Put one up and people stop to find out what's so important that a rope is needed to hold patrons back. Soon a crowd forms. The crowd draws more passersby as everyone wants to know what's going on and if they can get in. If they can, they may not even question the huge cover fee, assuming that it will all be worth it.

Another example of social proof is Chuck, a guy I knew in high school. Chuck was smart and spent a lot of time researching home stereo systems. He read all the *Consumer Reports*, reviews and shopped around for the best price. When Chuck pulled the trigger and bought a system many others followed suit, assuming he knew what he was doing. Chuck became an *influencer*.

These techniques are how social media works. When Chuck posts a product he likes on Facebook, his friends purchase it because they trust Chuck. Ashley is the restaurant expert and her reviews influence many of her friends to select or avoid a particular restaurant. Influencers can drive a large amount of business towards you, or away from you. And the velvet rope trick? Google launched Gmail as an invite-only service, making many of us wonder how we could score an invite. Nice!

Another reason social media works is because people like to share information.

People share online:

- To bring value
- To entertain
- To define themselves
- For self-expression and self-fulfillment
- To market their causes or brands

I know you have received a humorous email and passed it on because you just knew others would love it, too. In that case you shared to entertain your friends. It's also interesting to note that humor is one of the biggest factors in sharing.

How Can You Find an Influencer or Expert?

I've had folks in the media tell me that they prefer to have people on their show or in their publication who have a lot of fans, friends or followers on one or more of the major social media sites. In other words, you could have a fantastic message, a great product or fantastic business, but you still might face an uphill climb if your social media numbers are low. It's a sad but true statement in our society, and everyone's marketing plan should include increasing your social proof. One of the best ways to gain access to influencers is to network with them on Facebook. Here's a quick tip to start building that synergy with big names: friend them or "Like" their Page and then send them a quick note, thanking them for their information or whatever it is they are contributing. Additionally, I always recommend doing an outreach to two Facebook friends or fans at least once a month—you can do more if you have the time. Send them a private message or post something appropriate on their Page. Yes, it's a lot of work but it's worth its weight in networking gold.

How Can You Use the Velvet Rope Trick to Create Exclusivity?

Make your Facebook Page invite only, or require approved access to a Group. I only recommend this if you have a big following or a super popular topic—in my view, you need momentum to start something like this. Yes, exclusivity rocks but you need the numbers to drive the interest and intrigue. Pinterest, for example, did this in order to get invited. They gave you a "wait time," but if you knew someone, you could get in right away. Because the site was getting a lot of buzz, this trick worked.

How Can You Get More Shares for Your Message?

We're going to dig into each of the social media platforms separately, but overall the goal is to be relevant, interesting and insightful. Don't just copy what everyone else is doing. Be unique. That's easy to say and hard to do, I know. But let's face it, the numbers never lie. When you put an article or blog post out there that gets a lot of buzz, you know you've hit your mark. In order to define how to make your content more relevant, try asking yourself the following questions:

- What does my audience really need?
- What's the biggest challenge my market faces right now?

- What's the biggest hot button my audience has?
- What's next in my market?

The above questions may or may not work for you, but it should give you some general guidance on where your content needs to be focused. It should be extremely audience-driven. In other words, it doesn't matter what *you* think, it only matters what *your consumer* wants. That's the key.

What Is a Social Network?

Social networks, also referred to as social media, are places where people can join and become members of an online community. These networks provide tools that enable members to configure a customized version of a user page; create profiles and bios; manage invites and contact lists; upload photos, video and music files; and interact with each other via multiple channels.

People join social networks for a variety of reasons: to socialize, share and/or self-promote. The one caveat to this is that social networks are not receptive to marketing messages or sales hype, but users on these sites are looking for answers and advice. So your presence on a social networking site should be about 80% education and 20% sales. Users on social networking sites are seeking friends, mentors, experts and guidance. If you can offer one or all of these things, you can certainly grow your list.

SUCCESS SECRETS WITH SOCIAL NETWORKS

"When I took office, only high energy physicists had ever heard of what is called the WorldWideWeb. . . . Now even my cat has its own web page."
— Bill Clinton

In general, regardless of the social media or social networking outlet, the rules are the same. Let's take a look at a few:

Who Needs You?

The goal of any social media campaign should be to pull people into your site and message. You do this by putting a helpful, insightful or trendy message out there. This sounds a bit nebulous to someone who is new to social media: "So, you just put it out there and hope people find it?" Not really. You go to where they are so they can find you.

Let's say you are at a big networking event. Thousands of people are in attendance, and you're there to market your business. Not everyone there will be interested in what you are promoting, so where do you begin? By listing the traits your ideal client has and considering like we did earlier in this book, you start by first identifying the folks who have a need what you have to offer. To further identify what your market wants, let's start with an exercise. Did you do this exercise? So, where do they hang out online? This is going to take some thought on your part and you may find that this list keeps morphing and growing. Once you have it though, I know you'll find it very helpful.

Let's say you sell custom silver bracelets. These are expensive items, so your clients have money. They travel often. They have an interest in Southwestern art. Wine drinking and hand-crafted tequila are big parts of their lives. Maybe their age range is thirty-five to fifty. They shop at upscale stores and last but not least are women (or buying gifts for women). The first thing you should do you is spend time, maybe several hours, online looking at custom jewelry sites. Make a list of these sites. Then go to art sites that cater to the Southwestern theme and find out what social media networks they have a presence on. Follow them on Pinterest, Twitter and Facebook and start dialoguing with them, sharing ideas, tips and information. Their users are your demographic, so if you're connecting with people through sites they frequent, you are reaching out to your exact right audience.

The Conversation Buzz

The growth of social media has changed the way we gather news and the way that news is absorbed and disseminated. When Osama Bin Laden was killed, before anyone broke the story or even knew what was happening, one guy who lived near the compound tweeted about helicopters buzzing overhead and loud explosions. He did this in real time, ignorant that a major historical event was going on.

This has become a normal part of the news cycle. Anyone with a cell phone can transmit the news worldwide via social media. In fact, to stop atrocities in places like Syria, governments are actually considering air-dropping millions of cell phones so the average citizen can video soldiers raping and killing them. The idea is that the world will be outraged and step in to stop it. Plus, when Johnny Soldier sees himself on TV shooting someone in the head, he and his buddies may stop. In Egypt, citizens used tweets and Facebook to set up times for protests. These coordination actions eventually brought down the government.

All of these tools change our media window from hours to minutes. In 2008, Motrin launched a commercial that moms found offensive. One mom in particular was really upset and decided to blog about it. Over the next few hours, the story took over the mommy-blogosphere on its own blogs, Twitter and social networking sites. Within 48 hours Motrin issued an apology and retraction of the ad because the online noise was simply overwhelming. Compare that to the story from just four years earlier about the Kryptonite bike locks that could be opened with a ball-point pen. It took 10 days for that story to reach critical mass before the company issued a full recall of their faulty locks. The news cycle is driven by the Internet in ways no one could have anticipated.

So how do you capitalize on this powerful force online? Well first off, to make sense of this online world, think of it as one big cocktail party. If you walk into an event where pockets of conversation are buzzing all around you, you're going to seek out the groups or conversations that interest you most and ignore the rest. This is what social media is: pockets of relevant conversation. Some you will participate in and some you won't. The choice is yours, and your objective is to find the conversations you want to participate in online and then make them part of your online marketing efforts. We'll go into "how" you do this in just a little bit.

There's a Lot of Noise Out There

Publicity and marketing have changed in ways that no one could have anticipated, and that's a good thing. Why? Because now we have lots of open channels that help us market. Could you imagine living in a world where if you didn't get traditional media or even a regional paper to pick you up, no one would ever know about you? I did, and I marketed in that world. Believe me, it wasn't easy.

Twelve years ago when I was first in business, it was unclear whether blogs would even make a dent in news and communication. Back then, if you wanted to promote something you had to advertise in radio, TV and print publications, otherwise your message would die quietly and all your efforts to launch your business would go with it. Cycle forward to 2012. We *live* online, and social media has almost replaced the nightly news.

And while it's great that we have these channels, this new, tethered social media world has a downside. We have lots of information constantly bombarding us. And not all of it is news, either. Some is just wasteful white noise and much of it we ignore. Now the challenge is not just getting someone's attention but retaining it. And can you keep their attention long enough to get them interested in your message and turn these contacts into evangelists? One thing I've learned: it's not a challenge everyone is up for, and that's okay. If it's not your thing to wrestle your way to the top of the Twitter posts or Facebook mentions, that's fine. But if you want to get noticed and sell product, you'll have to up your game. I will explain how as we dig deeper into this book.

Understand the Time Commitment

All of this takes time. At my company, we know how tough it can be to stay on top of or get ahead of trends. Trust me, it's worth the time you'll spend. But if you're drowning in email newsletters and daily news bulletins, here's my recommendation: Set aside fifteen minutes each day to go through all your industry announcements, tweets, publications and Google Alerts.

Red Hot Tip!

What Are Google Alerts?

If you're not familiar with Google Alerts, head on over to http://www.google.com/alerts**. Once you are there, you can input any name or keyword you want to track. The system will let you know when your search term appears in the news or in blog posts. And here's another tip: make sure to get these on your name, product, business or book, and add your blog URL because some folks may cite you listing only your blog address.**

Next remember that the first word in social networks is "social." These networks only work if you interact with them. I'll profile some of the major networks in this chapter so you can get an idea of what "being social" means.

Whenever appropriate (and this will vary from network to network), join groups, be sociable, be interactive. Participate. You can't just show up at a party and sit in the corner. Well, you can, but you probably won't get asked back.

Think of social networks as an online party or network gathering. You'll want to be out and networking as much as you can.

If you can spend a half an hour to an hour a day on your networks, that's great. Don't overdo the time you spend on them or you'll burn yourself out. If you can use the social network feeds to have them syndicate your blog to the site, the updating of your social networking page will be done for you, to a greater degree anyway. You'll still want to get in there and tinker, update content, add friends, etc.

Tight Focus

As we continue to delve into this new world, you'll start to see more niche social networking sites like those built for wine lovers, car lovers and book lovers. Sites like Goodreads and LibraryThing are great examples of niche sites. Both cater to book lovers and see millions of hits per month. Their extraordinary growth has led to many publishers developing entire campaigns around promoting their authors on these sites almost exclusively. The more focused a site can get, the more the network expands. And how many sites should you be on? As many as are appropriate to your message and you have time to manage. If you've got a book about cars, then by all means, join the car-lovers network. Got a book about travel? There's a travel-lovers social network as well (we've listed a few of these niche networks later in this chapter). The tighter the focus, the better chance you have of reaching a lot of folks. But keep in mind that you don't want to be on a site just because it's niche. If it's not active, it's likely not worth your time. Be selective. Don't just be everywhere, be everywhere that matters.

What Can Social Media Do for You?

Now that you understand the ability to accurately spread information lightning-fast to many people at one time, how can you get more exposure and publicity for your business, get more people to talk about your book, product, service or brand and sell more of what you are offering? Here's how: It's not enough to get mentioned in the news. While it's great, that alone won't sell your stuff. You have to get in front of enough people in a very interesting and unique way. You have to get them to fall in love with your message so much that they'll talk about you, tweet about you, Like you on Facebook and tell all their friends to go buy whatever it is that you're selling. The new world of publicity is really about the consumers and the message. How will you get your community so enamored with your message that you turn contacts into evangelists? That's the new PR (Public Relations, in this case—not Page Rank). And I will cover everything you need to know about Facebook, Twitter and StumbleUpon in this chapter. These three social media sites will provide an excellent foundation for your Internet publicity strategy. First up is the big daddy of them all: Facebook.

The Facebook Factor

Facebook has a great feature that most users don't even think about. Remember when I talked about the first websites and how hard they were for a non-techie to change? Even today they are not simple. If it's hard to change, then you won't likely change it. This means it won't have fresh content or news. Not with Facebook. You can change it in seconds by posting a status update. That's the point I want to make: Stay current with your product. If you have a book you are promoting and you have a book signing coming up, bingo! Add updates letting everyone know where it will be. When it's over, post photos of the event.

Be Good or Be Gone

For lack of a better term, there's a lot of junk online. A lot of people ramble on about things that only they care about. We currently run a program that gets a lot of "Likes" to a client's Facebook Page. We're such a numbers-driven society that people love this program. Here's the kicker though: You can get Facebook "Likes," but that doesn't mean they will keep on liking you. You have to post good, interesting, unique and compelling content. If you ramble on about the flight you missed or the bad day you're having, I can guarantee that people will turn the virtual channel. There is so much information out there, you must be good or be gone. You won't even have to leave the virtual party, because if you keep posting self-absorbing, look-at-me posts, no one will listen anyway.

No One Cares What You Say

Truth be told, no one cares what you tell them. A survey done by Edelman Digital noted that fewer than one in three people trust marketing messages. Scary, isn't it? People only care about what their friends say, who their friends recommend and how their peers see them. You must be so compelling, interesting, funny, helpful—or whatever—that people will start to evangelize your work. That's when it happens: When you become interesting enough that people want to tell other people about you.

Numbers Matter

Let's face it; we're a society that pays attention to the numbers we see on Twitter and Facebook. If you are promoting yourself and have ten followers on Twitter and sixteen "Likes" on Facebook, you might want to think about paying more attention to these sites. Consumers like what other consumers like, and the numbers associated with these sites often determine how "likable" you are. Bigger numbers get consumer (and media) interest.

Do Stuff People Will Love

Getting people to love you is easy: Do stuff they'll love. This is why I talk so much about giving away information, being helpful and being on top of your industry. I am always stunned when people come up to me at conferences to tell me how much they love our newsletter (*The Book Marketing Expert*) or how much they love the information we share on Huffington Post. Give people what they want and they will give you what you want: Love (and, hopefully, sales).

Do Stuff People Will Hate

Not everyone will love what you say, and that's okay. When I wrote "Why Some Authors Fail" (http://www.huffingtonpost.com/penny-c-sansevieri/why-some-authors-fail_b_534629.html) I thought everyone would hate that piece. It turns out some people did, and that's okay. I once had a good friend and business coach tell me: "If everyone loves you, you're doing something wrong. Embrace it."

Stay on Top of Current Trends

This is a big one for most of us. We're out of touch, out of ideas and out of time. Staying on top of current trends seems like it's just another time suck. But trust me, it's not. Remember the Google Alerts I suggested you set up? Use them to gather ideas on new topics to blog on and new developments in your arena. Staying topical is important, especially if you're trying to keep someone's attention.

The Profile

Years ago, before social networks, we met people in clubs, organizations and bowling leagues. We may not have had "profiles" like we do on these social networking sites, but the concept was still the same: Like attracts like, and similar interest-based people gather in places that support their common interests.

For some authors I've worked with, the idea of exposing their profile online is scary. All sorts of questions come up relative to safety and identity theft. But aside from the predator element that would exist with or without the social network, these sites are pretty safe as long as you use caution when filling out your profile. We'll go into more about creating your profile later, but for now know that social networking can be safe and fun and doesn't have to be a way to expose all the details of your personal life.

Gain Their Trust

There's an old saying that goes: Fake it till you make it. But in social networking you can't fake anything. The best sites are those with an authentic voice. Social networkers can sense an individual who is pretending to be just an "average Joe," but is really looking for a quick sale. In fact, the worst thing you can do is constantly promote yourself.

Users join social media sites to socialize, not to buy stuff. As we migrate through this chapter, it's good to remember that. Be helpful or be gone. That's the motto of the social networks. Remember that social media (much like anything on the Internet) is a trust-based model, and you gain trust by helping, advising, educating or enlightening your readers. Seth Godin (sethgodin.typepad.com), one of the gurus of Internet marketing, (who started a social networking site called Squidoo.com), is a great example of what to do when promoting yourself. He offers helpful advice, tips and insight but rarely promotes his book. Does he sell books? You bet he does, but he's helpful first and a salesperson second. The point is, gain someone's trust and you'll probably gain a sale too.

First Order of Business: Your Message

The first piece of gaining trust is to figure out what your message will be online. If you're going to expose details of your life, figure out what you want to expose—or, I should say, what's necessary to expose in order to get your message across. This is important because once you start branding yourself on the 'Net, you want to be consistent.

THE FACEBOOK FACTOR

"During my service in the United States Congress,
I took the initiative in creating the Internet."
— Al Gore
(He later said: "The day I made that statement I was tired because I'd been up all night inventing the camcorder.")

Among the social networking sites, Facebook is probably the best known of all. Facebook was founded by Mark Zuckerberg in February 2004 at Harvard and was originally designed as a hobby project. Within a few months it spread across the college, and shortly thereafter Facebook sign-ups extended to Stanford and Yale. Since that time it's grown in numbers no one could have anticipated. In fact, there has been such a change in traffic and demographic that the average age on Facebook has changed to a median 35-64.

Keep in mind that there are a few different activities you can do on Facebook. A Profile is the standard way to get yourself onto Facebook if you're just starting out, but if aggressive promotion is what you seek, then a Page or Group might better suit your needs.

Facebook Profile

This is where it all begins, with your Profile. If you have one, you've probably been using it for personal contact, family photos, etc. But if you're running a business, consider now expanding into a Fan Page, which we'll cover shortly. If you're in a Profile and you want to continue using that as a marketing vehicle, you can make some simples changes that I'll explain in a minute to still preserve your privacy and deliver special updates for friends and family.

Facebook Pages

Pages were launched by Facebook in November 2007 as a way for businesses to establish a brand presence on the site. Pages are a lot like Groups, with some important differences:

- Pages are more customizable than Groups. You can add HTML, Flash or even Facebook applications to your pages to extend their functionality and the depth of experience users can have with your brand.

- Pages get more prominent "branding" real estate than Groups on the Profile pages of your fans.

- There is no limitation to the number of fans in your group that you can message.

- "Fans" who join your group are *not* able to invite their friends to be fans of your Page. Fans must either "Share" your Page with their friends or their friends must observe that they "are a fan" of your Page either via their Profile Page or News Feed.

- Facebook has taken an active role in cracking down on Pages not created by authorized agents.

Pages are a good option for small or local businesses that want to establish a presence on Facebook. Like Groups, they're another free and easy way to do viral marketing.

Facebook Groups

Groups allow you to control delivery of your information to select people. For example, if you have things only co-workers should see, you create a Group for them. When you make a post on your Wall, they will see the post and not your friends. Groups are restrictive in that they limit who can see your information. This would seem counterproductive to getting more Internet publicity, but it can fit nicely into your plan. Earlier I mentioned the velvet rope trick. Here's another example: If you are selling jewelry, you may create a Group for your special clients to see items first, before anyone else. This exclusivity can really work for getting clients excited about your product or service.

Personalize

Facebook works really well when your Page is personalized, so add some applications that will further enhance this Page. You'll want to add photos, a library where you can select books you're reading or ones you recommend. You can upload video and add content from your blog. You goal is to making the Page as robust as you can.

Widen Your Reach

Start building your network by looking for friends, colleagues and Groups that are appropriate to what you're doing. Join any Groups that seem to fit your message, and start networking.

Don't Be Shy

The purpose of Facebook is to connect and interact with other members, so don't hide in a corner! Interact with people on your friend list by commenting on their pictures, commenting on their news, or wishing them a happy birthday. Doing all these things will help others get to know who you actually are instead of just knowing your name.

Content, Content, Content

Remember that it's important to frequently add content your reader will care about. You can also add Facebook applications such as notifications from Pinterest, Twitter and YouTube so that your Page stays populated with relevant content.

Slow and Steady Wins the Social Media Race

The best Facebook Pages (and this is true for any social networking site) are built over time. A slow build is best when it comes to social networking sites, so don't force a sudden surge of growth. This will also keep you from getting booted off if you add friends too quickly. Facebook watches for people who are adding hundreds of friends at a time and will lock your Page if they think you're over-promoting yourself.

Add Your Facebook Page Widget to Your Blog

Make sure to add a social signup (your Facebook Page Like box) to your blog. You can have your web person take care of this for you. It's a simple widget that gets added to let people know you have a Facebook profile.

Paid Advertising

If you choose to pay for advertising, Facebook Pages are an extremely cost effective method compared with the well-known Google ads. Facebook lists these options:

- *Advanced Targeting* – Target by age, gender, location, interests and more.
- *Content Integration* – Get noticed, not skipped.
- *Flexible Pricing* – Buy clicks (CPC) or impressions (CPM).
- *Trusted Referrals* – Attach friend-to-friend interactions about your business to your ads.

If you want to do some inexpensive advertising to extremely targeted markets, you can sign up for a paid advertising campaign for your Facebook Page. As always with Facebook, make sure you comply with the Facebook Advertising Terms of Service (http://www.facebook.com/ad_guidelines.php).

HOW TO USE YOUR PERSONAL FACEBOOK PROFILE AS A MARKETING TOOL

"The attention span of a computer is only as long as its power cord."
—Author Unknown

Before I launch into this section, let me be clear: Facebook Profiles should never be used for business/marketing. That said, I've used my Facebook Profile to connect with others and offer helpful guidance, and it's worked extremely well for me just as it can for you. Just remember, no selling.

When we work with clients, they often come to us with Facebook Profiles that have lots of friends but with Fan Pages that don't have a ton of fans. Yes, you can try to move them over—in fact at one point Facebook would even let you migrate people from your Profile to your Fan Page, but privacy laws have forced Facebook to remove this feature.

The biggest problem most people face with a personal Profile is that they have a lot of content that's, well, personal and most people want to keep sharing personal information. So what I'm going to suggest is segmenting information out because that's the best and only way to capture some additional people to your message, and perhaps also fans to your Fan Page.

How to Separate Your Content on Facebook

So, let's look at how you can segment out your lists, personal and public. With all the Facebook changes and updates, it's actually pretty darned easy to do this. Let's have a look.

First up, you want to allow subscribers to sign up for your public updates. If you haven't set this in your account, now is the time to do so. Head to *Account Settings* and then click *Subscribers*. The Page should look like this:

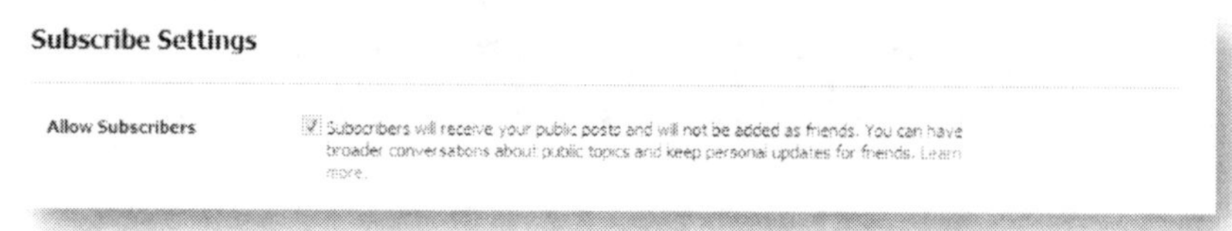

When you've done that, head on over to your photo albums and set the privacy settings there, too. Like this:

Managing Your Account Settings

Once you are in your account (you've clicked on *Account Settings*), on the left-hand side toward the bottom it says "You can also visit your privacy settings."

This will take you to where you need to go next and allow you to control each post as it's added to your personal Profile.

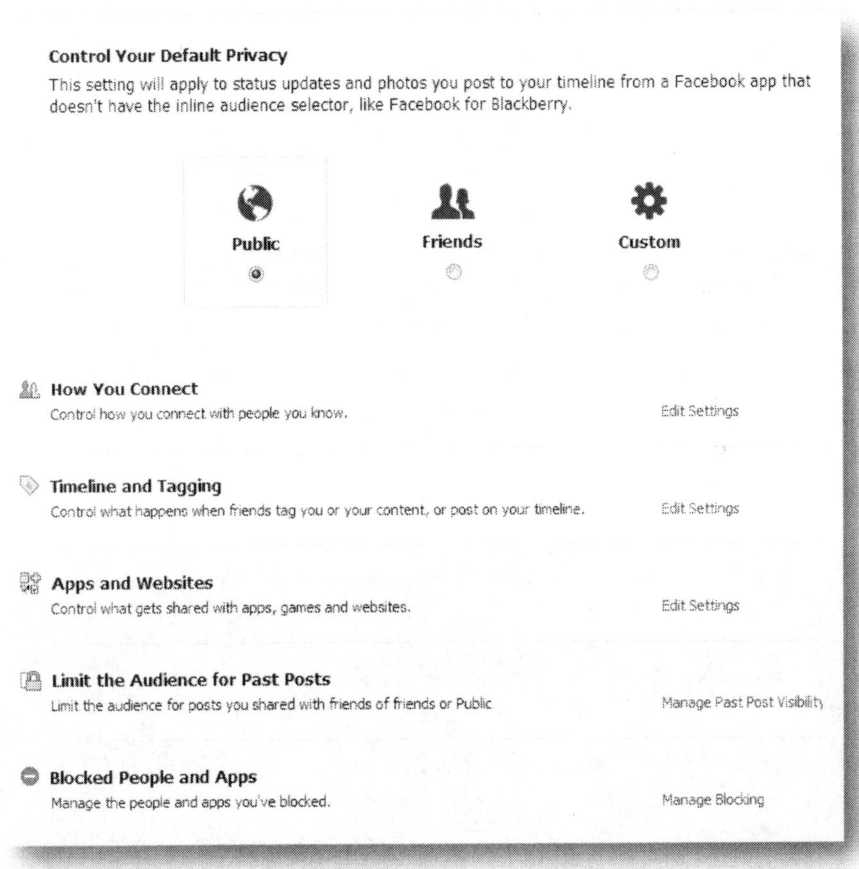

You can also modify your personal Timeline settings so that this information is only visible to friends. But if you're going to use your Profile for networking, why wouldn't you want people to learn more about you? I leave my settings public, but you can decide what works for you.

This way, you can keep your personal information private. I would suggest keeping things like your website listings public so people can always get to your business, blog or other websites.

Now to Update

Now that you're ready to use your personal Profile for networking purposes, you'll want to post helpful information like links to articles, helpful tweets, videos and any other content that your consumer might benefit from. Remember to be helpful, not salesy.

And finally, one of the biggest benefits to using a personal Profile is that the updates tend to show up better in the News Stream, and it only takes four Likes and four comments to rise to the top of the News Feed. One of the things I'll do on my Facebook Profile occasionally is go to Someecards.com and create something funny, or use a quote around my area of expertise. People love quotes and they love humor, so you can do this to help drive more engagement to your Profile Page, and therefore get more exposure. Just be sure that when you're posting material that you want public, modify each of those status updates to push the content out publicly. If you have your security set to keep your updates isolated to your friends, you will need to modify each public update as you post it.

Red Hot Did You Know?

Some amazing Facebook facts:
Monthly active users now total 901 million
3.2 billion Likes and comments are posted daily
300 million photos are uploaded to the site each day
Daily active users are up to 526 million

THE MYTH ABOUT BEING "LIKED" (ON FACEBOOK)

"A computer lets you make more mistakes faster than any invention in human history—with the possible exceptions of handguns and tequila."
— Mitch Ratcliffe

These days it seems everyone is after "social proof"—that elusive number of "Likes" or followers that will make you seem part of the "in crowd." Unfortunately, getting someone to like you is only half the battle. You must now get them to stay "in Like" with you. With 42 million Pages on Facebook, how will yours get noticed?

Studies show that the expectation of content does vary by age, but the direction is still the same: It's more than just getting someone to Like your Page; you now must learn how to keep them. With all the social media options out there, it's critical not just to build numbers but to maintain them too. In order to do this, it's important to know what users want and when they want to see you post new content.

As I pointed out earlier, content expectations vary by age. For example, Facebook users between the ages of 18–26 have the lowest expectations of receiving something in exchange for their Like endorsement. When you go up the next rung, ages 27 to 34, they are more likely to expect something solid delivered in a Facebook update. But the users with the highest expectations, and those you are likely serving, is the 35–51 age group. This is also the group most likely to Unlike a brand if it fails to meet expectations.

Create Engagement

But it's not only about having great content; it's also about creating great engagement. A study done by Roost.com evaluated 10,000 Facebook fans across 50 industries and found that certain posts leverage more engagement than others. Here are some of their findings:

- Photo posts get 50% more impressions than any other type of post.
- Quotes get 22% more interactions.
- Ask questions to spark dialog. Questions generate almost twice as many comments. But keep your questions easy to answer. Yes or no responses will get better traction than questions that require long, lengthy answers.
- Fill-in-the-blank posts tend to receive nine times more comments than other posts.

Timing Is Everything...So Be Concise

Now you have the content down, and you know about the types of posts that will get more play than others. But is there more to successful posting than just content and post-type? You bet. Timing of posts is also important. Here are some quick tips on how to improve your Facebook Wall posts:

- Posts delivered between 8:00 p.m. and 7:00 a.m. EST tend to receive 20% higher user engagement.
- Best day for Fan engagement is Wednesday: 8% higher.
- How many posts does it take to increase user engagement? If you're thinking more frequent posts, you are wrong. Posting one to two times per day produces 71% higher user engagement than posting more frequently.

- When it comes to Facebook, more is not better, sometimes it's just more. Posting with 80 characters or less receives 66% higher engagement. Very concise posts of 1–40 characters generate the highest engagement.

Finally, users do vary. How can you really know if your fans are engaged with your content?

Understanding Facebook Content Interaction

Fan Pages now have a fabulous feature called Facebook Insights. Head over there to see some really interesting and insightful (hence the name) data. First, you can find Insights under the *Help* tab at the top. Look under *Create and Manage Pages* for *Page Insights*. You have to have at least thirty Likes before you can open up the full range of Insights, but once you're there, you can see all sorts of data on the information you post:

- *Reach* – This is the number of unique people who have seen the post for 28 days after publishing it.

- *Engaged Users* – These are people who have engaged with your post in some way (i.e. clicked the link).

- *Talking about this* – This is an interesting number you've no doubt seen this pop up right under your Likes. These actions are: Liking the post, commenting, sharing the post, responding to a question or RSVPing to an event.

- *Virality* – This is the number of people who have created a story (i.e. shared your post with their friends) from your Page post.

An example of Facebook Insights

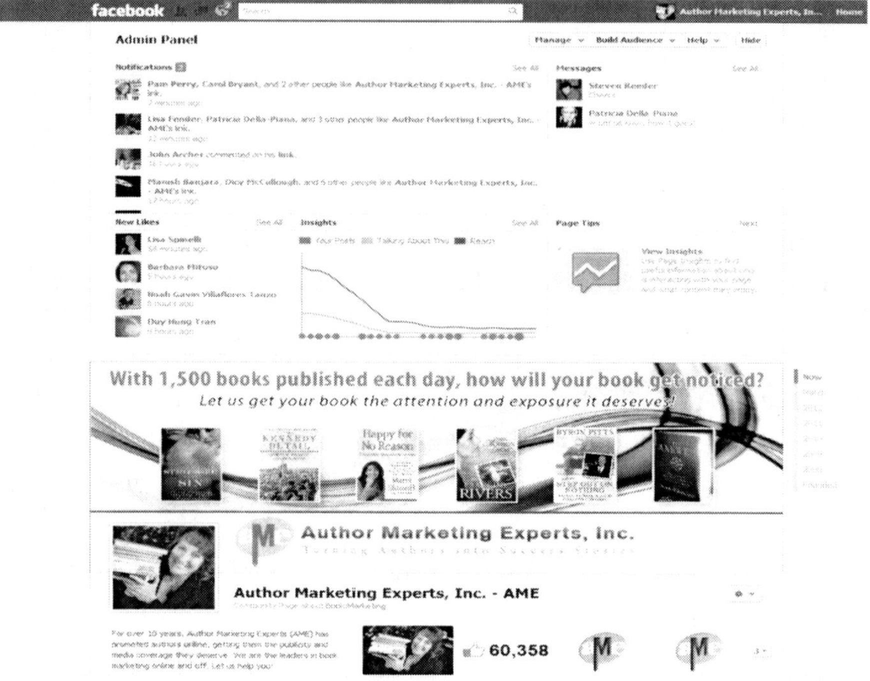

Watch these numbers for some great insight into what fires up your fans and what leaves them cold.

> **Red Hot Did You Know?**
> **Did you know that only status updates with 4 Likes and comments make it to the Top News section of anybody's News Feed?**

Stay Liked

It's not just about getting "Liked," it's about staying "Liked." Creating insightful, helpful and engaging content is one piece to the puzzle. The other is timing and receptiveness of your fans. Though I've outlined general user guidelines in this chapter, be sure to check the Facebook Insights for key data that will help your fan base thrive.

- **Likes:** It almost goes without saying that the more Likes you have on your Facebook Fan Page, the more appealing your messages are. As I have said several times (and I want to make sure you get this), it's about more than Likes, it's about engagement. You can have 30,000 Likes on a Fan Page with very little engagement. The reason for this? There are a lot of people out there who can help you build a lot of Likes, but these Likes are essentially from dummy Pages, which mean that there's nobody managing them. There's no live person at the other end of that Page. The other reason for this is that without engagement, your Fan Page just looks static. Engagement makes it much more interesting and conversational.

- **Facebook shares:** Make your content interesting enough and people will share it. You want to get to the point where each of your posts is being shared at least once. How do you do that? You create content that is insightful, helpful and unique.

Facebook Facts:

- **1 in 13 people on earth is on Facebook.**
- **70% of all USA Internet users are on Facebook.**
- **It has more than 845 million active users.**
- **The average Facebook user has 130 friends.**

MARKETING ON TWITTER

"On Twitter we get excited if someone follows us
In real life we get really scared and run away."
— Author Unknown

When Twitter first launched on the scene in 2006, it was referred to as a micro-blogging platform, but it was originally designed by a group of friends to communicate via text messaging, hence the length of the tweets (140 characters). Since that time, it's become so pervasive that it's even spawned its own vocabulary. Terms like tweets, hashtags and others weren't even part of our language three years ago. Now even my dog has a hashtag (well, not really, but you get the idea). Twitter has been exploding for several years now. In addition to using it to keep in touch with friends and family, Twitter can also be a great place to share your latest project, promote discounts on your products as well as interacting with fellow "tweeters" or "Twitter peeps" (folks on Twitter).

When Twitter first started, people were a little perplexed, and many first time tweeters just didn't get it. I mean, why on earth would you want to blog in 140 characters? Consider this:

Here are a few Twitter facts:

- There are over 465 million Twitter accounts.
- If Twitter was a country, it would be the 12th largest in the world.
- 30% of Twitter users have an income of more than $100,000.

You likely know what Twitter is, or have heard of it even if you've never been on it. If that's the case, check out this easy-to-understand YouTube video, Twitter in Plain English: http://www.youtube.com/watch?v=ddO9idmax0o.

Do You Speak "Twitter"?

If the Twitter-language confuses you, check out Twittonary.com/. It has every possible Twitter-term you'd ever want to know.

Why does Twitter work so well? When I think about what has really pushed Twitter to be a must-have especially when pursuing Internet publicity, it's that fact that you *cannot* exceed 140 characters. That strict limit assures your tweet readers that they will be able to read the message in just seconds. Less sometimes really is more.

Signing Up for Twitter

To sign up for a Twitter account just go to Twitter.com and complete their short sign-up form. Remember to brand yourself! This is important. Another important tip is to not let your name run together (i.e., have a space between your first and last name).

Here's a screenshot of what I mean by having a space between your first and last name.

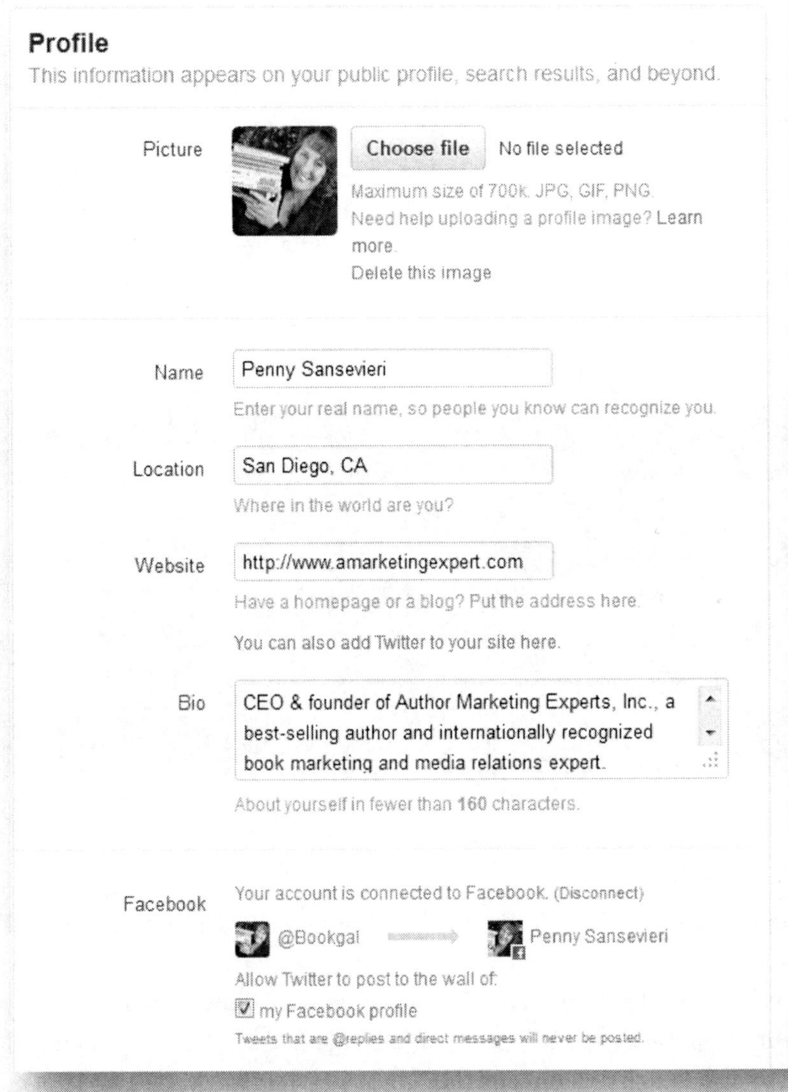

Why is this significant? Because it'll help you come up in searches. If I had listed my name as pennysansevieri few people would find me because they don't search for me that way.

Next is your actual handle on Twitter, whatever it is, make it functional to your brand. So maybe it's @fictionwriter or @careercoach or whatever you want. My Twitter page is @bookgal (note that all Twitter names are preceded by an @ when referenced on the site). You can also find me at twitter.com/bookgal. This is a fun play on words for what I do (and what I love). I don't recommend that you use an underscore (so stay away from Michael_the_Consultant) since underscores can be tough to remember and if someone is trying to tweet to you from their cell phone, iPhone or whatever, those underscore keys can be tricky).

Also, be sure to have a great, sharp bio and a link back to your website. Very important. This small addition could help send a lot of traffic back to your account.

Red Hot Tip!

Looking for local Twitter peeps? Try these sites:
Nearbytweets.com
Twitterholic.com
TwitterLocal.net
Twellowhood (twelow.com/twellowhood)

Don't Give Up

Once you have a Twitter account you can immediately start tweeting. The service is completely free, and you can keep up with other people's tweets by "following" them. Their tweets will show up on your Twitter home page so you can easily keep track of them. You can also be notified by phone when they add a tweet, though I don't recommend this. Once you start following a lot of people, these constant updates can get mind-numbing. Remember that you can tweet from anywhere, even your iPad and phone.

Don't feel bad if the first time you go to Twitter it seems like a mess of conversation. Most people feel confused when they first enter Twitter-land, and many don't see the point. When I made my first entrance into micro-blogging, none of it made sense to me. It seemed a bit useless. But then I got the hang of it and saw the real benefit to having and managing a Twitter account. That's really the key. Much like any social media tool we've discussed in this book, it's more than just having an account, you have to manage it, too. But give yourself a little time on Twitter before you give up on it. At some point it'll either all make sense or it won't. Either way you're only out a few hours and, perhaps, a few informational tweets.

> **Red Hot Tip!**
>
> **Would you like a custom Twitter background? They are easy enough to create. Just head over to one of these fun sites:**
> **TweetStyle.com**
> **Free Twitter Designer (www.freetwitterdesigner.com)**
> **Twitbacks.com**
> **Twitter Gallery (www.twittergallery.com)**
> **Have fun!**

Use Popular Words

When you write tweets, using keywords can help your tweets be found by others much faster. Though keep in mind, that you should pick keywords only as they relate to your topic. When you're trying to decide which words you want to use, you can see what's hot right now on Twitter by checking out Twitscoop.com. Look under their *Hot Trends* tab to see what everyone is tweeting about. Another great site that recently went down but may be back up is TweetVolume.com, which will give you the ranking of keywords you want to use. Just plug in your search term or terms and up pops a list of results!

What's a Direct Message?

This is a way to send someone a message privately on Twitter, precede it by "dm" (without quotes). You can only send Direct Messages to those who follow you back.

Feed It

Yes, you can have a blog and a Twitter page. I have both, but I feed my blog into my Twitter site so that my Twitter page gets updated each time I add new content to my blog. There's an easy application to add your blog feed to Twitter, it takes just minutes to do. Head on over to: Twitterfeed.com. Why is this important? Because people search for information on the Internet and they can find your posts easier with the more places your posts reside the easier you are to find. Twitter will shorten down the information and then send it out for anyone to see. If a searcher picks up your shortened tweet, they can simply click on the link in the tweet and be taken to your actual blog post. Easy! And don't forget to feed your other sites like Facebook, LinkedIn and Pinterest into Twitter, too.

Red Hot Tip!

Most Influential News Media on Twitter:

1. People Magazine @peoplemag
2. CNN @cnn
3. The Wall Street Journal @wsj
4. Harvard Business Review @harvardbiz
5. BBC Breaking News @bbcbreaking
6. Time Magazine @time
7. Good Morning America @gma
8. Reuters Top News @reuters
9. Mashable @mashable
10. CNN Breaking News @cnnbrk
11. The New York Times @nytimes
12. Fox News @foxnews
13. Newsweek @newsweek
14. The Economist @theeconomist
15. Fast Company @fastcompany
16. USA Today @usatoday
17. CBS News @cbsnews
18. Us Weekly @usweekly
19. ABC News @abc

The Power of the Retweet

Retweeting is how a person on Twitter shares a tweet. Retweets are preceded by RT, so they're easy to spot. Why are they so powerful? If you post great tweets that get retweeted, you gain the exposure not just of your Twitter peeps but of the retweeter's too. For example, we once had a client who was on Twitter and we were managing his campaign and he got retweeted by Honda. As you can imagine, with Honda's hundreds of thousands of follows, that was significant because now his message was viewed by many more people than he originally had access to. That's the real secret behind a RT. You may only have a hundred followers, but if someone who RTs you had millions...well, you get the idea.

You might not get a hit as big as our previous example, but if your posts are helpful they will get shared. Getting shared and sharing other posts is key to Twitter!

Here's what a retweet looks like.

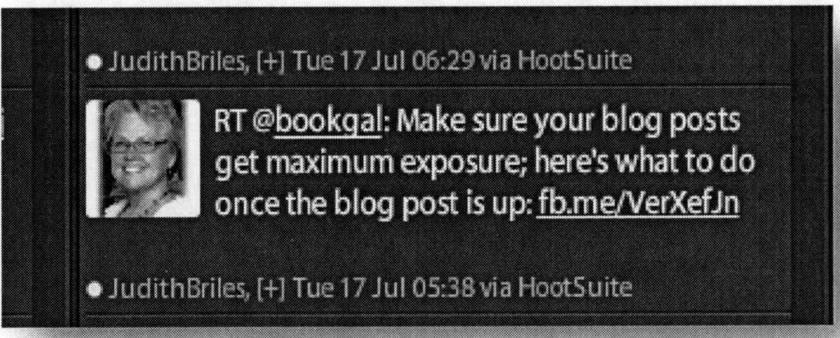

What's Follow Friday?

When someone sends a message using the #followfriday or #FF hashtag, they will usually include a username. So, for example, #followfriday @bookgal. Follow Friday is a fun hashtag that you can use for recommending folks to follow. When someone does it with your username, be sure to thank them.

Widen Your Network

Follow other Twitter folks. This will not only give you some ideas for your own tweets, but it's a great way to network with other folks in your industry. The key word is *network*. Don't expect your followers to grow if you're not following other people. Search for big names in your industry/market on Twitter and follow them. This will do two things, bring in their followers and tell you what the "big guys" are up to. And while you're at it, visit Twitterholic.com to check out the most popular micro-blogs on Twitter based on followers. To see how popular you are and how you rank in the grand scheme of Twitter fame, check out TweetStats.com. This will tell you if you're a Twitter hero or big zero. You can also use sites like TweetLater.com or Twitter Search (http://twitter.com/#!/search-home) to see who's talking about you and then follow them or comment on their tweets. Networking works. Really.

Red Hot Tip!

What's a hashtag? A hashtag (#) was created to help searching and indexing of tweets. You can view hashtags and in particular popular hashtags by going to Hashtags.org/. In simpler terms a hashtags is like a keyword or phrase to help with a search. Creating a hashtag is simple, but check first to see if it's in use. This doesn't mean you can't use it, if it's for the same topic that's great, but if you're using a hashtag for a different topic than what most of the tweets are about, you could end up with some confused followers. Additionally, you should use hashtags whenever you can to help drive more traffic and exposure to your tweets.

Here's an example of a Twitter peep using several hashtags in her post.

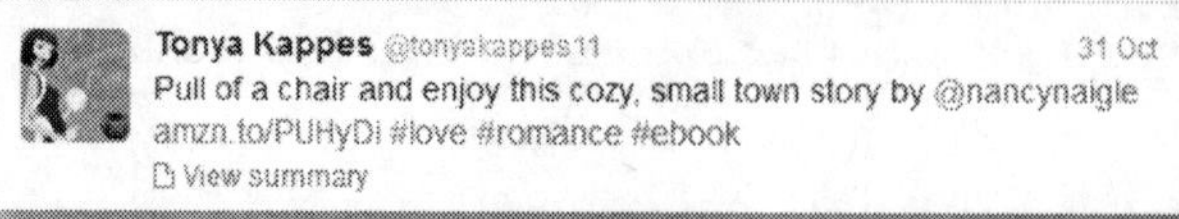

Offer Advice

When you land on one of these sites, don't ask "What can this site do for me?" Instead, ask yourself, "What can I do for the folks on this site?" Twitter (and any social media site) should be 80% helpful information and only 20% selling—; in some cases this percentage should even be smaller. If you flip this percentage (so 80% selling) you will get very few followers and even fewer leads from Twitter.

When I started tweeting on other helpful blogs and websites and linking to my own articles that I'd syndicated on the Internet, my followers doubled and tripled on a daily basis. Another trick I learned was to offer advice. Once I started offering advice and I saw how effective it was, I began looking for people who were *asking* for advice. TweetDeck.com and Twitter Search are great ways to see who's asking for info on your area of expertise.

When I plug in my keywords and respond a few times a day to questions people pose on Twitter and offer helpful advice, my followers increase. Don't feel like you have to respond to every tweet, but I generally try to respond to all tweets that are replies to mine (you can find these under @replies on your Twitter home page). When you find them, offer some help or insight. This is a great way to build relationships.

What to Tweet?

Be original, useful and helpful. It's okay to market yourself but be careful about pimping your stuff too much. Every tweet counts so don't tell people you're washing your cat. And don't just tweet on useless stuff or you'll lose followers. It's not all about you (again, back to the cat). People want to know useful stuff. I know, I'm getting repetitive but there's a reason- it's important! Even though I said not to post useless information, it's still not a bad idea (from time to time) to post a personal tweet or two. Provide value and Twitter-followers will beat a path to your door.

You may start out with plenty to tweet about, but eventually the well can run dry. To stay on top of your market and find stuff to tweet about, go to Alltop.com and search for your category. Created by Guy Kawasaki, Alltop is a great place to go if you're short on ideas. There are literally thousands of categories you can sift through. Find the one or ones that make the most sense. You can also look at Stuff To Tweet (www.stufftotweet.com), Daily Mashup (www.dailymashup.com) and Digg's top in 18 hour list, which is a listing of their most popular stories in the last 18 hours (found by clicking the Popular button on the Digg.com site) for some top stories that are making the news.

Finally, quotes tend to do well on Twitter, so don't forget to post those occasionally, too.

Multimedia on Twitter

Are you ready to add pictures to your tweets? Twitter does not let you store multimedia on their servers, so you have to use a third party site. Twitpic.com lets you upload pictures to their servers and tweet from them. Videos can also be shared with Twitvid.com. Music on Twitter is also possible thanks to TwittyTunes (http://www.foxytunes.com/twittytunes/), which is wonderful for sharing music and it has a simple Firefox add-in that lets you tweet music you're currently listening to.

Twitter Warning

I was a little surprised when I recently read that you can buy Twitter followers on the Internet—something like 2,000 followers for $10. In order to do this you have to share your login information. I don't know about you, but I would be a little hesitant to give my login to someone on eBay. Tempting, but potentially disastrous. Still, having a large number of Twitter followers does matter, and there are ways to do this without handing over your ID to some unknown person: it's called work.

Twitter as a Pre-Event Networking Tool

Twitter can be a great way to network with speakers and participants prior to going to any event. Virtually any conference or tradeshow now has a hashtag. I recommend following that hashtag prior to the event. (in fact you can even create a separate search for it if you use a service like Tweetdeck, Hootsuite or SocialOomph.) Then every time someone tweets with that hashtag, you can comment or retweet them. Also, if you have some folks you're eager to meet, go ahead and tweet to them using the hashtag so it stays part of the conference or event conversation and they know you're going to be there.

Networking on Twitter

Aside from following a hashtag, I also recommend that you build lists on Twitter, which you can do right from the Twitter page itself.

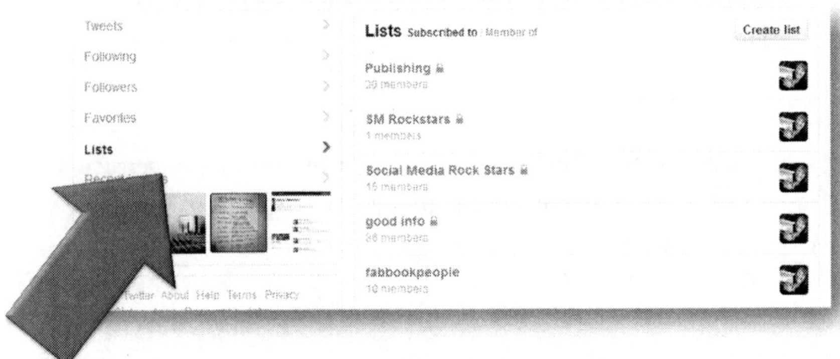

You can isolate Groups, and I recommend doing this for particular niches. Then when someone from that group posts a tweet, it's easier to spot because they are grouped together.

Get More Followers – More Red Hot Twitter Tips

If you've pondered using Twitter but aren't sure how to do it effectively, here are some tips:

- Teach stuff. - teach a little mini-lesson on Twitter. Delve into your area of expertise. If you run a BMW repair shop, just talk about BMW maintenance and how to make minor repairs to a BMW.

- Share sites or blogs that your followers would be interested in. Be their filter to new and exciting information.

- Use SocialOomph.com to add tweets to your account for later posting so you don't have to be sitting on top of Twitter every minute of the day.

- If you want a local following, try logging onto Nearby Tweets (www.nearbytweets.com). It's a bit of work but a great source for driving local traffic. Another great local site is Twellowhood.com.

- Use Twitter as a news source. You can easily announce news both from your world (as long as it relates to your topic) and from the world of your expertise. For example, I've done tweets on book industry happenings and breaking news on eBook publishing.

- If you're attending an event promoting your product or service, tweet on that and invite your local followers to attend. Also, Tweet any good reviews your product or service gets. It's always fun to share the good stuff.

- It's okay to repeat your tweets. With the volume of messages people get, your followers will often miss some of your posts. Don't make it a habit to repeat all of your tweets, though you can try repeating Monday's tweets on Friday.

- Promote your Twitter account in your email signature line and on your blog.

- Embed a link or some other signup in your welcome message. This is another great way to capture emails for your newsletter (assuming you have one).

- Join http://twitter.com/#!/petershankman for tweets on media leads. (It's a great service!)

- Review a product or book on Twitter.

- Get a good picture of yourself. Don't leave your avatar blank. Personalize your page if you can, but a good Twitter picture is a must.

- TweetBeep.com is a lot like Google Alerts. You can plug in your keywords and you're pinged each time they are used.

- TwitterMail (http://twittercounter.com/pages/twittermail/) supplies you with a personal email address. If you send an email to that address, it will be posted to Twitter. Not sure what to tweet about? Check out these creative profiles: @celebritygossip; @cookbook; @books.

I have entire articles written on getting more engagement on Twitter, but the bottom line is this: If you get more dialed into your topic, do more networking on Twitter, comment on other people's tweets, share them and include hashtags in your posts, you will build your followers. The idea is that becoming numbers-focused really forces us to develop more relevant content. And the numbers never lie. I once did a Twitter mentoring for a business owner who started with five followers on Twitter. She loved Twitter but wasn't sure where to go with it. We researched her audience, dug into their needs and then pushed a timely, interesting and helpful message out there. Now, a year later, she has 68,000 followers on Twitter.

MASTERING LINKEDIN

"The Internet is just a world passing around notes in a classroom."
—Jon Stewart

For years many of us didn't pay a lot of attention to LinkedIn, but by 2012 this site had grown to 161 million professional users. Though LinkedIn's primary base is in the United States, the site is seeing traffic from all over the world. In a recent article, Forbes called it the "must have" in corporate recruiting. But what if you're not looking for a job or interested in hiring—can LinkedIn still benefit you? Yes. Let me explain why.

LinkedIn will never be Facebook, nor does it want to be. While Facebook offers a variety of ways to share news both in personal and professional formats, LinkedIn is much more buttoned-down and professional. The site is designed for business networking only, so save those new puppy pictures for your personal Facebook profile.

What LinkedIn Offers

With LinkedIn you can get an account for free, or you can pay a small monthly fee for an expanded account and access to members. With the paid subscription, you can reach members who aren't in your network with LinkedIn's email system called InMail. For now though, we're going to focus on the free profiles. Most people on LinkedIn use the free profiles quite successfully.

Red Hot Did you Know?

Who's the biggest and baddest on LinkedIn? Check out: http://www.toplinked.com/toplinked.aspx

Getting Set up on LinkedIn

LinkedIn is really an online résumé, it's a place to showcase all of your talents, skills and products or services.

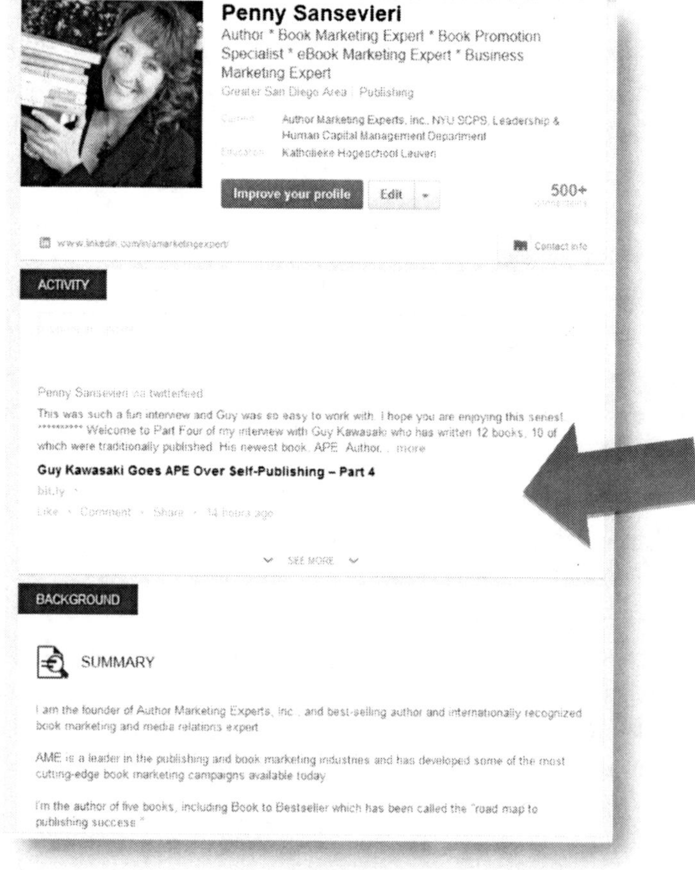

Here's a snapshot of my profile to give you an idea of what a LinkedIn profile typically looks like. Note the arrow pointing to my status update—we'll talk about that in a minute.

Red Hot Tip!

Be sure that your picture on LinkedIn is good, clear (not pixelated) and professional. You probably won't want to use your Facebook picture here, but you might. Just remember this is a professional site and a great place to showcase your business.

You have the opportunity to use keywords all throughout your profile and you want to take advantage of that because keywords, especially in the LinkedIn searches, will help you come up higher in search results. Find ten to fifteen keywords to use and then put them in your job title to start. Mine used to say "CEO" which was, frankly, boring. Wayne Breitbarth, author of *The Power Formula for LinkedIn Success* coached me on using keywords here instead. Now you'll see my title has numerous attributes to it.

Below your profile will be your summary. This is important and will likely change often as you change, enhance and grow your business. I recommend using keywords in this area, too, so people can easily find you when they are searching for professionals on LinkedIn.

Below the summary is an area for specialties. Here is where keywords really come in handy. As you're putting this together, keep in mind how people search you. What words do they use? You should be using those words, too. If you've done a number of jobs within your job, be sure to break those out. For example, I teach for NYU and I added that as a separate piece within my profile. I'm also an author, so I added that as well.

Finally, be sure to make your profile public. You'll have the option of keeping it private, but I don't recommend it.

Marketing Tips for LinkedIn

- *Be the Expert:* People love working with experts, so position yourself as one. Showcase your expertise. You can do this not only on your profile but by joining LinkedIn groups and answering questions and posting helpful information. You should also visit the LinkedIn answers section and respond to members' questions. It's a fantastic way to network within LinkedIn. Ready to join some groups? Head on over to www.linkedin.com/groupsDirectory to find more folks to network with.

- *Get Recommendations:* Another useful piece to LinkedIn is the ability to get recommendations from people you've worked with or done business with. I recommend that you gather as many recommendations as you can within LinkedIn. It can help enhance your page.

- *Find People to Network With:* When you find members you want to add to your connections, send them a quick note in LinkedIn. Their default message reads: "I'd like to add you to my professional network," but I highly encourage you to personalize this. Just a sentence or two is fantastic—when you send a slightly more personal note, it feels like you've done your homework and aren't just adding connections for the sake of growing your numbers.

- *Update Your Status:* Whenever you update your status on LinkedIn, it will also let you send these updates to the group or groups you belong to.

Red Hot Tip!

Remember that your profile can help attract not only new business but also some key media contacts. You can easily network with media folks on LinkedIn by sending them an invite and networking with them there.

Sharing Information and Becoming an Expert

Sharing Information: Since LinkedIn recently broke up with Twitter (meaning you can no longer use Twitter to feed your status updates), you'll need to find other ways to share content. You can head to: http://www.linkedin.com/static?key=application_directory to find all sorts of applications like SlideShare (which we'll talk about in a minute) and a WordPress app that lets you run your blog posts through LinkedIn. This is a great way to keep content moving on your LinkedIn profile.

SlideShare: If you have lots of presentations (or even just a few), a great way to share them is via SlideShare.net. You can activate the app on LinkedIn, and any slides you upload to SlideShare will get shared there too. SlideShare is a great tool anyway because it grabs the attention of consumers looking for content. If you do a lot of speaking, and even if you don't, create PowerPoint shows and upload them there to teach or share insights.

Groups: I've already talked about this, but it's worth mentioning again. LinkedIn Groups are a fantastic way of networking with others in your market. Join a few groups and start following the conversation and posting content. Stay as active on these groups as you can.

More LinkedIn Tips

- Keep your status updated. According to a recent report by Lab42, only one-third of LinkedIn members visit the site each day. This means that the people who stay active remain in the feeds.

- Comment on profile updates of people or companies you follow. If you can do this once a day, great. If not, a few times a week is a great way to stay top-of-mind.

- Keep building contacts. You should do this daily or at the very least weekly. Your objective on LinkedIn is to keep the new connections flowing. LinkedIn continually makes recommendations on your page, so be on the lookout there too. Most of the time their recommendations are spot on.

- Be active later in the day. Studies have shown that activity on LinkedIn peaks in the afternoon and evenings, (for those accessing the site on mobile) so plan your updates accordingly.

Making the most of LinkedIn isn't hard; it just takes a bit of effort and a different approach than Facebook or Pinterest. But if used correctly, this professional site can benefit you in fantastic ways.

GOOGLE+

"Google earth:You can go anywhere on Google earth and the 1st place you go to? Your house."
— *Unknown*

Recently Google announced that Google+, their new social networking site, reached 250 million users. Though that number is staggering, keep in mind that these aren't all active users, just folks who have registered for an account. Therein lies one of the biggest challenges with Google+, the accounts are easy to register for. If you have any access to Google at all (and who doesn't these days?) via their applications such as Gmail, Google Drive and others, you're going to get into Google+ almost by default. The problem is that most of us, once we're there, have no idea what to do with this new social networking platform.

Many SEO people tout this social networking site as a "must" for search engine ranking, and we pay attention because it's Google. Of the 250 million users that Google cited, there are only about 75 million are active, far less than Facebook. But here's the kicker: when you're in Google (so using Google products), you'll always be "in" Google+ because of the way Google has set up the notifications. Have you seen that red box in the upper-right-hand corner of your screen when you're in Gmail? That's your Google+ notification letting you know there are new updates for you to look at. And while Google+ is still relatively new in the market, users spend on average of twelve minutes per session, per day on Google+, which is only down by eight minutes from Facebook.

Google's objective with Google+ and their other applications is not to become "just another social network" but rather a core ecosystem because their systems and services are vital to doing business (think Gmail and Google Drive). Google has also rolled out a new tablet which has an Android operating system, much like smartphones.

How Google+ Works

With Google+ you can use Circles to isolate who you want your news to go to. You can have friends and family Circles, work Circles for work friends and so on. This allows you to cherry-pick the information everyone sees, like we talked about in the section on Facebook profiles. Google+ was designed to do this, realizing that not being able to customize the information people see was a flaw in the social networking system.

If you have a gmail account, you can gain easy access to Google+. Once you're in there you'll see the *+You* in the upper-left-hand corner. Click on that and you're in! Then you'll be able to upload your picture and a banner (similar to the Timeline feature in Facebook). Now let's take a look at the individual features of Google+:

Hangouts

One of the first things to get a lot of buzz was the Hangouts. Literally you can "hang out" with two, three or ten people with these remote online video chats. You can also stream live to YouTube (via Hangouts on the Air) and record these sessions. Google Hangouts has hundreds of great applications. Consider:

- *Customer interaction* – Invite your customers to "visit" with your team during these planned sessions. Folks can pop on and off, ask questions and engage with you and/or your team. You can also showcase products or even do live demos. We do these monthly—sort of a meet-the-publicist. It's fantastic and always well-attended. People get a chance to ask questions, get answers and even network with other folks on these video chats. (To get on the list, email us at info@amarketingexpert.com.)

- *Behind the Scenes* – Consumers love to see the inner workings of companies they buy from. Why not take them on a tour via Hangouts? It's easy enough to do with a wireless connection.

- *Live Expert Interviews* – Bringing in an expert is often a great way to build content and give valuable content for your clients. Bring in an expert, invite your customer base and start streaming!

- *Meetings* – We are an entirely virtual company, meaning everyone is everywhere. Using Skype became prohibitive because of connection issues, and also they charge if you have more than two people on a video chat. Enter Hangouts, a great way to stay visually connected. Sometimes we'll even do client calls this way. We work with people all over the country, and it's great to be able to meet them, albeit virtually.

There are quite a number of applications being rolled out for Hangouts, including SlideShare, Scoot & Doodle and Google Effects. Did you create an awesome Hangout? Submit it to Google (https://support.google.com/plus/bin/request.py?contact_type=hoa_submit) and if they decide to use it and promote it, it could be some great exposure for your business.

Using Circles

As I mentioned earlier, Google+ has allowed you to segment out your contacts. When you sign in, they'll give you some pre-named Circles to choose from, but I recommend having some fun with these. Rename them and add new ones.

Tips for Using Google+

- *Tagging* – You can tag anyone in your circles by using the + sign before their name. Similar to the @ symbol on Facebook, they'll be notified of your posting.

- *+1 Button* – This is Google's version of Liking a post. So the more +1s you get, the more popular your post. You can also +1 someone else's posts by simply clicking that button.

- *Pages* – Pages on Google+ are directly connected to search, so along with a profile you should also have a company page, which is simple to set up once you're logged in. Keep in mind that searches for keywords can turn up your pages in Google+, so be sensitive to keywords in your About descriptions.

- *Be Unique* – One of the things that sets Google+ apart is the benefit of unique content. In many cases I will cross-post updates to Facebook, LinkedIn and Twitter, but generally not to Google+ because this site, even more so than the others, thrives on fresh, new content.

- *Content* – Marc Pitman of The Fundraising Coach suggests that you post entire blog posts to Google+, rather than just their links. He asserts that entire postings get more attention.

There's still a lot to learn about Google+ and new features are being added every day. One thing is for sure: Google is serious about their social networking site and is investing a lot of time and energy into this platform.

I spent some time with Matt Beswick of Quirkle, a web design and SEO company, and he offered the following insight as an SEO expert about Google+:

1. Why should we care about Google+? What makes it different from any other social network out there?

We should care because Google cares. They've been "playing" with their own social network for what feels like forever, but Google+ seems to me like the real deal. There are rumors of a Facebook search engine, whisperings that users are slowly but surely going to move away from traditional search mechanisms and a feel from pretty much everyone that social is "the future." Google needs to be there and getting left behind just isn't an option for them.

2. Is there a real SEO benefit to Google+?

If we think of SEO as generating targeted traffic to your site, then yes. As it stands there's no ranking benefit to using Google+, but with "Search Plus Your World," the combining of Google Places with Google+ and the addition of people you have in your Circles below URLs that they've given a +1 there's loads of reasons that Plus will help with search traffic. This is only going to increase as time goes on, too—social signals are going to become far more important to rankings, so you really need to get ahead of the curve.

3. Is there a particular type of person that could benefit more from this site?

The joke at the moment is that the only people who use Google+ are Google employees and SEOs. A tad harsh maybe, but it's not that far from the truth. Having said that, a good friend of mine runs a travel site in South Africa and has had great success by posting images and local travel advice (although he admits that he's not quite sure how or why).

4. How often does it need to be updated and what type of content works well there? I read somewhere that people on Google+ don't want to click off the site like they do on Facebook—they want all the content there, which suggested that posting entire articles in Google Plus is acceptable. Is that true?

It's like anything "social"—you need to be consistent, pick your niche, interact with the right people and post as often as you can (without being annoying). I've never heard the comment about posting entire articles to G+, and to be honest it sounds like a pile of rubbish. As long as you're posting great content to your profile, people will be more than happy to click through to it.

5.What are some tips for getting started on Google+?

Don't have expectations that are too high. Sign up, start posting regularly and use the search function to find relevant people in your niche. 'Circles' (friend lists) are really handy as you can segment who sees what you post... so for example, you could have a circle full of Pet Bloggers and one of SEO Professionals. All you need to do then is remember to tick the right box whenever you post something.

6. *If you had a crystal ball, what would you predict for the future of Google+ and all its partners (YouTube, etc.)?*

I expect Google+ to succeed, but there's a long road ahead. The important thing to remember is that Google as a whole isn't going to go away, and they're going to continue pioneering how things are done online no matter how much the likes of Facebook wish it weren't so. The advantage they have is the range of products and offerings: it's nearly impossible for anyone to catch up with them. I can see everything becoming more integrated, though, and it wouldn't surprise me if at some point Google looks to tie YouTube and Google+ together somehow. It would be the perfect way to give a quick (massive) boost to mainstream traffic.

STUMBLEUPON

"The message for business people contemplating their place in cyberspace is simple and direct: get linked or get lost."
— Vic Sussman and Kenan Pollack

Many of you may be familiar with StumbleUpon, a Web 2.0 site, but I don't think many people know how to use it effectively. StumbleUpon's allows you to discover sites based upon "word of mouth." The idea is that it will make recommendations based upon the personal preference of like-minded surfers. This is a very important aspect to get traffic to your own site. A record of your "Stumbled-Upon" sites can be found in your generated StumbleUpon blog.

You can definitely get a lot of traffic to your website or blog if you know how to use it correctly, because there are over 25 million StumbleUpon users. For such a young site this is great! And remember, traffic equals Internet publicity. Here are some ways to drive that traffic higher.

Setting Up Accounts and Categories

Who says you can only have one account? No one! You should have one account per major topic. Do you sell more than one category of product? Are you a consultant in many different areas? Do you write both nonfiction business books and also romance novels? Set up one account for each category. There are categories that you can pre-select, using StumbleUpon and this is important for the type of market you want to get into. You'll need a new email address for each new account but that's easy to obtain.

Your Title Is Everything

Just like the headline of an article, the title of your website attracts attention. It should contain keywords and be compelling. Your best bet is to see what sites your "friends" are recommending and create a similar style.

Copycat

Model your landing page to already popular StumbleUpon sites. If you look on a person's favorite website list, you can see what people have recommended in the past. Use that to your advantage. Model your website after them, making it similar in structure, layout, etc.

Choose Your Friends Wisely

StumbleUpon will let you create your own social bookmarking page and choose friends with similar interests. The first thing you want to do is add friends who are interested in the market you want to get traffic to. (Makes sense, right? You *do* have to know the market you are targeting.) So, if you are selling wine, only select friends who are interested in wine (you can select categories or just search for a specific topic) and then recommend they StumbleUpon that site. There are StumbleUpon groups are available that you can join with similar interests and you can get almost instant traffic that way if you join a popular group. The more friends you have, the more traffic you can get. However, the more friends you have that are interested in your topic specifically, the more targeted traffic you will get—and that's what you really want.

Consider Video

One super tip that will help you build a list quickly is to create a page that has video. StumbleUpon users like video. Create a teaser video on your site and call that "Part 1." Then say, "If you'd like to see Part 2, just enter your name and email address." Actually what you are doing is just breaking up your video, showing the first few minutes, and to see the rest you can tell people to put in their contact information. Voila! You are building a targeted list to stay in touch with.

Advertise with StumbleUpon

You can advertise your website with StumbleUpon at https://www.stumbleupon.com/pd/index/redirect-ads/. Your website gets an increased weight (i.e., more impressions on others' StumbleUpon pages the likelihood that your site will be stumbled upon) over someone who is submitting for free. Right now they have three tiers of pricing. Check it out.

It does take a while to get a campaign to work and it can take up to a week for you to get approved. But if you can be patient, there is a good chance it could be quite worthwhile.

Bottom Line: Create good content and emulate already successful StumbleUpon sites. The key to success with StumbleUpon is to build a site that people *want* to stumble upon.

POWERFUL PINTEREST

"Getting information off the Internet is like taking a drink from a fire hydrant."
— Mitchell Kapor

Back in 2011, I listened to Gary Vaynerchuk talk about this new site called Pinterest. Though I didn't get it, he was really excited about it and insisted, "Get on Pinterest now!" I didn't listen, thinking "Oh, dear, not another social network!" But Pinterest has proven to be anything but another social network. First, its growth has been extraordinary. According to several reports, including a blog post shared on Mashable, from September–December 2011 unique visitors on Pinterest increased by 429%. That kind of growth has never been seen in a social network, and while it's still early for Pinterest we're seeing a lot of staying power, especially with established brands like Macy's, Land's End and magazines like *Real Simple*—which got more traffic from Pinterest in October 2011 than from Facebook.

For those of you who haven't been on Pinterest, the concept is almost deceptively simple. You sign up for an account (there's a waiting period right now as Pinterest tries to manage traffic and new accounts, once you sign up it should take about a week before you can get in). The site is a collection of boards, like virtual bulletin boards that you name and add to your page. You can have as many boards as you want and name them whatever you want (though make sure to read through the Pinterest terms of service so you know you're not violating any of their regulations). The boards can describe your brand, book, message or business. We'll look at some board ideas in a minute, but for now think bulletin board.

So, that said, how can you make the most of Pinterest and obtain some Internet publicity? Like any social network, I recommend that you poke around, follow a few people in your industry and see what they are posting about. There are a lot of creative boards and a lot of companies using Pinterest as a unique brand extension. Check out http://pinterest.com/chobani/. They have all sorts of boards that tie into their brand, including Chobani Champions, recipes, spoons and sans yogurt which is a board about all things non-yogurt related. Now, that's how you do it!

Setting up Your Pinterest Page

The set up is changing as Pinterest grows, but right now it's so simple you shouldn't be hard pressed to figure it out. When you get to the profile, be sure to add a catchy description to grab others' attention. Also, when you're setting up your Pinterest account, link it to your Facebook and Twitter accounts, too. This will help you gain followers. Don't forget to add the icons to your profile page so you can direct people there, too.

Picking Your Boards

Like your profile description, it's important to come up with creative and interesting board names. Keep in mind that these board names get shared whenever someone re-pins you, so make them catchy! When you first start on Pinterest, you are a completely blank slate. It's up to you to fill your new Pinterest page with exciting boards. But where to start? Well, your business, product, message or book will often determine the boards you put up. The idea is that whatever you are promoting, you can create a board to support that. But you need good content.

Creating Compelling Content

You should consider your audience first and what they would like to see. Here are a few ideas:

- If you do a lot of speaking or other physical engagements, create a board that captures the excitement of these events by posting pictures and videos. This is especially great for any conferences you're attending. You could put the board up early with "teaser" content to encourage sign-ups too.

- Create a customer or reader board that has pictures and/or videos of happy customers. I often talk about capturing endorsements or reviews on video when you see someone at an event. These can be posted to this board. Thank you boards are an interesting twist on this, too.

- How-to boards are great as well. You can create a board (or several) around a "how-to" related to your product or service. This might include training videos related to the products people purchase. Tutorials are big for our company, so we plan to offer tutorial boards to help walk our clients through how to use social media, how to continue reaping the benefits from our campaigns once they are done and other compelling information.

- Company boards are popular—ones that showcase your company, sharing your core values and highlighting your team or any behind-the-scenes stuff related to your company. You can always use these to showcase new products.

- Trends and seasonal stuff make great boards. So don't hesitate to create a holiday or trend board if you think your audience will be interested.

- You can also let your customers work on a board with you. Create a user-generated content board and invite customers or readers to pin away! Just let your imagination run wild and see if you can come up with some fresh ideas.

Need some ideas? Click the "popular" link on Pinterest to see what's hot and what's trending. You might be able to make this a part of your content strategy.

Engage

Make sure to engage on Pinterest. Re-pin and comment on pins you love, and since you can see pins from folks you aren't even connected with, be sure to broaden your reach when networking. You never know where the next follower will come from.

Photos and Video

Pinterest loves videos. Think about what videos you can pin to a board. When you blog, be sure to include great pictures so that when you pin your blog post to your board you can capture a great image. Images on Pinterest are hugely important.

Keywords are big on Pinterest, so be sure to think carefully about what you name your picture and what words you use in the description. You can even use hashtags on Pinterest, and if you're trying to get the attention of another pinner, use @ followed by their username to tag them. You can also use $ to add a "ribbon" to your pin that will immediately show pricing. This is great if you're selling a product.

Spread the Word

I mentioned this above, but I want to make sure you do it. When you add your pin, don't forget to tweet it and add it to Facebook. You can do this as soon as the pin is loaded. Be sure to promote your Pinterest account on Facebook, Twitter, on your website and in your email signature line.

Sample Boards

Here are some good boards to get ideas from:
http://pinterest.com/societysocial/
http://pinterest.com/pulpwoodqueen/

Pinterest is a fun, if not highly addictive way to start marketing. Still not sure what to do? Then get started by following others in your industry and get a sense of what they're doing. The future of Pinterest is still uncertain—as we've seen in the past, social media sites come and go and (on occasion) get eclipsed by bigger, better, more creative sites (Pinterest itself stole some of Google's thunder from their Google+ launch)—but the site has grown at rates that no one expected and continues to do so. It's also been the quickest social media site to monetize—less than one year, compared to five for Twitter. Thus, Pinterest has already become a staple for many businesses.

THE KLOUT FACTOR

"I will not be impressed with technology until
I can download food from the Internet."
— *Unknown*

For many, Klout (www.klout.com) has become the website everyone loves to hate. How can one website rank our "influence" and, for that matter, should it? In 2008 Klout began to score social media influencers online, meaning that it would rank your importance based on your activity on sites like Facebook, Linkedin, Four Square, YouTube and others. So, the more active you are, the higher your Klout score. The higher your score, the more "valuable" you are as a social media influencer. But that's not all, Klout also assigns "perks"—freebies and goodies—to those with high Klout scores (often scores of 55 and up will get perks, but it also varies depending on your industry). Klout scores are also a bit oddly calculated so, for example, Justin Bieber's Klout score is 100 while the President's is 91. It's not a matter of personal influence; it's entirely based on your activity online. One caveat to this is that Klout recently updated their algorithms to encompass how someone influences offline too. For example, if there are two people at a company who are equally active online, the President or CEO will rank higher than someone who isn't a C-Level person.

So, why should you care about Klout? First, because Klout scores are considered by companies you may do business with and by employers who may consider hiring you. Second, because while you may not even have heard of Klout, it could still be influencing your life. Everyone who is online has a Klout score, and someone might be looking you up without your realizing it.

No one really knows where Klout will end up. It could become something that matters long-term and could affect things like sales, speaking gigs and an employer if you're in the market for a new job. There are quick ways to get started, and we'll cover that in a minute, but let's first look at some quick tips for gaining more exposure on Klout increasing your score:

1. *Be active* – That's possibly the #1 way to attract a higher score on Klout.

2. *Link up your sites* – Make sure and add your various social media sites to Klout. Facebook is particularly important to your Klout score.

3. *Be a topic specialist* – Klout's influence centers around topic experts. So it's important to find your area of influence and use that work in your posts. Assess the topics you are keyed in on and then use those keywords to gain higher ranking.

4. *Big guns* – Getting to know other influencers in your market is important, not just because they are bigger influencers but getting them to share your content go a long way to helping your Klout score. Are you following your influencers? If not, you should be.

5. *Keep it current* – Klout doesn't have a long memory, well it does, but it doesn't rank you that way. Anything that you did more than 90 days ago doesn't matter on Klout; the system is keyed into current activity only. This is good because regardless of where you are now, a week can make a huge difference. Don't believe me? Try powering down on some of these tips for a week and see if your score hasn't changed. I'm betting it will.

There are a lot of ways to get better ranking, but oddly getting someone to give you a +K isn't one of them. Much like endorsements on LinkedIn and "+1" on Google+, Klout has a similar feature in its +K, their version of an endorsement, but it has no bearing on your overall Klout score. What does? Your activity online and your social influence.

Susan Gilbert, who writes extensively on Klout (she herself has a Klout score of 68) offers a few additional thoughts:

There are goodies offered on Klout. Why do vendors do that?

Since Klout is a social influence measurement tool, Klout Perks is another way that brands and individuals can be recognized. It is also a method for companies to target and reach out to a specific niche. When a company offers a perk to you on Klout, they are factoring in your score, what topics you rank in and your location. Klout offers this service for a large fee to companies that wish to use Klout Perks to reach out to potential customers and clients.

What are the steps for activating your Klout account?

When you are first starting out with Klout, it is very simple to set up your profile and make connections. Log into Twitter or Facebook then go directly to Klout's main page. You will see a button for either network. Choose one. Next, customize your profile, including your photo and description, which can be taken directly from your existing social media profiles. Klout will show you influencers to connect with and topics to choose for your niche. Complete your setup by connecting all of your social networks for improved ranking.

Do you think it's true that Klout may be the new credit score?

The standard credit score measurement is most likely to stick around a while, but the recent increase in companies using Klout to attract customers and offer incentives is on the rise. Klout is not an exact science, but this has not stopped large companies from offering special discounts to people based on the size of their social media influence. Their goal: To spread the word on their product and service. It is too early in the game to determine whether Klout's scoring algorithm will supersede credit scores. Large numbers may not be a great payoff for marketers, who also need to be careful not to push too much commercialization in a social-driven community.

PART FOUR:
RED HOT BLOGGING

"Describing the Internet as the Network of Networks is like calling the Space Shuttle, a thing that flies."
— *John Lester*

BLOGGING: THE SECRET SEO TOOL

"Give a person a fish and you feed them for a day; teach that person to use the Internet and they won't bother you for weeks"
— Author Unknown

What's Blogging and Why Should I Care?

Originally, there were these online journals called web logs. They were simple to use, which meant easy to add new content for others to see. They quickly became very popular as users journaled everything going on in their lives. People began saying weblog really fast and eventually the "we" was dropped, leaving us with *blog*.

Journaling is how these blogs took off, but if you're only using them for journaling you're missing the bigger picture. Blogs are not for the narcissistic or self-absorbed. They are instead helpful, useful and newsworthy insights into your product, your service, your work or your message. And the best part? When it comes to getting better ranking on your website, blogs are a fantastic tool.

Today there are over 180 million blogs, with over 100,000 new ones being added on WordPress every day. Collectively, they are called the *blogosphere*, an interconnected community of rapidly changing information. Some blogs are informative and some are just a downright waste of your time. Many are nothing more than a daily glimpse into someone's life, while others are so sophisticated it's hard to tell them apart from an online news service. Having a blog serves a number of purposes if you do it correctly, but we'll go into that later.

Though there may be massive numbers of blogs out there, the news is not all good. Technorati reports that about 45% of the blogs it tracks are not updated more than every three months—if that. An estimated 200 million people have already stopped writing their blogs. And did you know? More than a third of all blog posts are in Japanese, and recently Technorati reported the most active blog in the world was in Chinese.

What does all this mean? Blogs are powerful if used correctly. The blogs that work best are those that are newsworthy, current, informative and insightful. Boring blogs don't get noticed and they certainly don't get commented on.

Another interesting effect of blogging is the long-term effects it has on the population and society. Even the staunchest anti-blog critics are amazed. Blogs are a form of "water cooler" info, just like the latest TV show (before TiVo allowed us to watch them at different times). Blogs and their immediate effect on our culture have quickly become more talked about than the latest scandal on *Mad Men*. Journalists who read blogs do so for fresh perspectives and new, unedited ideas on a story. Also, blogs tend to rank higher on search engines than traditional websites, so they're easier to find. Consequently, partnering with bloggers (besides having your own blog) should be high on your list of things to do when promoting yourself on the 'Net. We'll look at this more in-depth in a minute.

Still not convinced you should have a blog? Well, consider this— an overwhelming majority of reporters and editors use social media sources for researching their stories, as 56% say social media is important for reporting and producing the stories they write, and 89% of journalists make use of blogs while conducting their online research (Cision & George Washington University).

Red Hot Tip!

Ready to drive more traffic to your site? Here's an idea: Interview someone influential. It's not only great content but it could be a great traffic driver too. When I interviewed Guy Kawasaki on our blog, our traffic shot up and nearly doubled for days after the interview posted.

A Blogger Profile

BlogWorld reports that the blog population has grown to around 12 million American adults, the equivalent of 8% of adult Internet users. The number of blog readers has jumped to 57 million American adults, 39% of the online population.

Technorati's State of the Blogosphere 2011 reports that there are essentially five different types of bloggers:

1. *Hobbyists* – The backbone of the blogosphere, representing 60% of bloggers, hobbyists say that they "blog for fun" and do not report any income. Half of hobbyists prefer to express their "personal musings" when blogging. Sixty percent indicate they spend less than three hours a week blogging, yet half of hobbyists respond individually to comments from readers. Because 72% blog to speak their minds, their main success metric is personal satisfaction.

2–3. *Professional Part- and Full-Timers* – Representing 18% of the total group, these are independent bloggers who either use blogging as a way to supplement their income or consider it their full-time job. Most don't consider blogging their primary source of income. This group primarily blogs about personal musings and technology.

4. *Corporate bloggers* – Corporate bloggers make up 8% of the blogosphere. They blog as part of their full-time job or blog full-time for a company or organization they work for. These bloggers primarily talk about technology and business. Seventy percent blog to share expertise, 61% to gain professional recognition and 52% to attract new clients. They have found that blogging has given them greater visibility in their industry and company. Most use number of unique visitors to measure success.

5. *Entrepreneurs* – Thirteen percent of the blogosphere is characterized as entrepreneurs, or individuals blogging for a company or organization they own. Eighty-four percent of these blog primarily about the industry they work in, with 46% blogging about business and 40% about technology.

Seventy-six percent blog to share expertise; 70% to gain professional recognition; and 68% to attract new clients for their business.

Google and Blogs

Google, the #1 search engine on the 'Net, loves sites that aren't static (i.e., that are updated/changed frequently), which means that it loves blogs. So much so that if you do it right, Google will spider the heck out of your site, pushing it right. What does it mean to "spider?" It's when Google, or the like, searches your site's content to establish ranking. The more content you have (i.e. fresh content), the more Google will do its magic and push your site up the search engine ranking ladder. Search engines also love websites that aren't static (i.e. have frequent updates like your blog does). Blogs generally have more incoming and outgoing links than regular websites, and these links (especially incoming) can have a significant effect on your ranking. Another reason blogs matter is that they are interactive, and if you blog on your product's topic it will help to further your expert status on a particular issue.

When we plan Virtual Tours for our clients, we include as many blogs as we can. Why? Because if you can get into a good blog that's seeing a lot of traffic, you can start to gain some exposure for your product.

Red Hot Tip!

Here are some great places to promote your blog and network with other bloggers:
MyBlogGuest.com matches guests with bloggers. (You can also search the site for blogs that allow guest posts.)
Submit your blog to BlogCatalog.com for added exposure.
Submit your blog (and even your website) to DMOZ.org for some great exposure. It's not easy to get into, but well worth it if you do.

Discover the Bloggers

How can you find these influential bloggers? Easy, head on over to a blog directory like Technorati.com and type in your topic, for example, wine. If you need to qualify it a bit more, such as finding the only white wines, then add a "+" after your search term so it looks like this: "wine + white." This will pop up more blogs than you'll know what to do with. Then start to find the right ones to partner with, blogs that mirror your topic that accept submissions or comments and bloggers that post on a regular basis. Once you've determined they meet this criteria, find a handful that you feel most passionate about, and post regular comments to the blogs they write. You can also send them an email asking for a backlink, pitching them a review or offering a freebie to their visitors.

Want to find other blogs? Here are some great places to do that:

Ask.com

Technorati

Google (http://www.google.com/blogsearch)

Icerocket

Red Hot Tip!

Here's a quick way to find blogs in your market. Start following your competition on Google Alerts. Just plug in their name, product or book and create an alert. Each time they appear on a blog, you'll know it's one worth targeting. Why? Because if you're following the top competitors in your market, you know that they likely won't spend time with blogs that aren't significant. This little trick can save you hours of research.

With a Blog, What Would You Talk About?

This is the question we get asked most often. "If I start a blog, what on earth would I talk about?" If you sell gardening tools, it's pretty easy to figure out what your topic would be. But if your sell just one kind of wooden window blind, it could get a bit tricky—but not impossible. In that case you would show photos of various projects, talk about where the wood comes from, how they are installed and maybe talk about beautiful windows you have seen even if they don't have your wooden blinds installed. This is a good example of why you need to spend time figuring out your audience's pain points as related to your topic. It will make the job of "what on earth would I talk about?" a lot easier.

In another instance, I may work with a client who sells life insurance. I will advise him to blog about stories where people had life insurance and stories where they did not. Readers may not like seeing a bad outcome and some blogs may be controversial, but that's okay. You want to create your own "voice," your own take on a certain issue, and if that opinion is controversial it's all the better for exposure and for getting people to interact on your blog. Getting readers to respond to your posts is a great way to gain interest and momentum for your blog, and (more importantly) getting people to talk about it will grow your blog like nothing else.

Here are some other ideas about blog topics:

- Talk about trends in the industry you're in.
- Review other (similar) products and services—this is a great way to network with other people in your market.
- If you are promoting a book, blog "in character"—readers love this!
- Ask readers for feedback on new products or services.
- Lend your voice to a "hot" industry issue or controversy.
- Comment on other blogs or feature other people on your blog.
- Interview people (other experts).
- Talk about the elephant in the room: If there's a looming issue in your market, offer your insight.

How to Start a Blog

Starting a blog is super easy. All you have to do is register at a blog site (like Blogger or WordPress) and get started. It's that easy. The blog service should link to your site; you'll need to ask your webmaster to add a button to your home page so people can find your blog.

Red Hot Tip!

To get the maximum optimization out of your blog I recommend two things: first, use WordPress because they seem to optimize better, and second, make sure that your blog is part of your website. Make sure it's hosted where your site is hosted. Your webmaster will know how to do this.

The Pieces that Make Up a Solid Blog

About Page

Did you know that the About page on your blog is one of the most read areas? Figuring out exactly what you should put there isn't always easy, but here are a few things to consider:

- What makes you an expert?
- Why are you blogging and what topics will you cover?
- What's the benefit to the reader?

Give some thought to enhancing and engaging your reader in your About page. It might make the difference between a regular reader and a casual observer. Whether you have a blog as a standalone or part of a website, the About page is really important.

Contact Info

The key is building relationships. The further we get down the blogosphere, the more and more I find bloggers are limiting ways to contact them. So when you post your contact details, make it count. Some bloggers have removed their contact information altogether because they found themselves spending their days sifting through emails rather than posting on their blogs. Most bloggers appreciate comments (especially those that aren't spam) more than you know. When you start your own blog, you'll see what I mean. Until then, I recommend adding your contact info. Be sure that the media or whomever can contact you.

Posts & Content

Blog posts are the individual topics you add to your blog. When you post a blog, the newest one will appear on the front page. When you post again, the new post will push the old one farther down the page. Eventually these posts will end up being archived. If you end up writing a lot of posts (and you should), the archives can get pretty long. With blog software like WordPress you can (and should) filter the different posts into categories—not just because it's helpful when you write a lot of posts, but it's also helpful to your reader if they are looking for particular content. The Author Marketing Experts blog is divided into several categories including marketing, publishing, newsletter archives, interviews, etc. Each of these contains posts on those particular subjects. It's a great way to keep your blog organized.

How to Blog Effectively

The best bloggers know that the more you add to your blog, the more traffic you'll drive there. Some bloggers I know post daily, sometimes even multiple times a day, while others post weekly. How much you post will probably depend on how much time you have to dedicate to this. The challenge is that if you want to keep driving people to your blog, you'll want fresh content.

This doesn't mean you have to create this all yourself. In fact, you can invite people onto your blog and interview them or you can just post a one paragraph "thought" on your topic. It doesn't have to be complicated or long, it just has to be fresh. Also be innovative, as we discussed earlier. Be different with your blog, have fun with it. It might seem complicated at first, but once you get the hang of it, you'll quickly become a blog expert.

Blogroll

A blogroll is a list of other blogs and websites that you recommend. This blogroll is somewhere on your blog, usually to the sidebar. You should always have a running list of your favorites and continually update them. Also, for each of the blogs you're recommending, take a look at their blogroll to see who they recommend. There might be additional bloggers or websites you want to connect to.

Red Hot Tip!

Tumblr is one of the hottest blogging sites out there. As of July 2012, it had 64.7 million blogs. If you just want to blog and don't want to be bothered with having a blog site, you can absolutely go onto Tumblr, but keep in mind that you won't get any SEO benefit or be able to sell products or collect emails.

How to Use Tumblr to Promote Your Blog

1. **Create an account at Tumblr.**
2. **Once you're in, click** *Text* **to share your blog in text on the Tumblr platform.**
3. **Type in your blog post title (I don't recommend changing this, use whatever post title you used in your blog).**
4. **Add a link back to your post.**
5. **Copy the text from your blog post into the Tumblr page.**
6. **Add tags (you can use the same tags you generated for the original post).**
7. **Hit** *Create Post* **and you're done.**

When you start going through Tumblr, you'll see that much of their posts are image driven. Using images on Tumblr is important, so consider using an image to promote a blog post—you'll increase your blog traffic using this effort.

Pinging

Now that you're going to all the trouble of writing a blog, you certainly want to promote it, right? Pinging is a way of notifying blog directories that you have a new post. It's sort of like having an assistant going to every blog directory on the web and telling them you've updated your content. If you're using WordPress as your blog platform, there's a spot under *Options* where you can list all of the sites you want to ping to. Let's list just a few of them here:

- Ping-O-Matic (www.pingomatic.com)
- Pingoat.net
- King Ping (www.kping.com)

You'll need to visit each of these sites and add your blog information when you start up your blog. Once it's submitted, every time your blog is updated, these sites will start pinging the blogosphere, letting them know you've got a new post.

Promoting Your Blog Posts

One of the biggest questions I get from business owners, speakers and authors is: "I have a blog but how do I get people to visit it?" First off, you want to keep blogging regularly (twice a week at a minimum), but there are other things you can do, too. We'll discuss two of the most powerful ones here.

If you've spent any kind of time online, you've probably heard the terms "tagging" or "bookmarking." But what exactly do these terms mean?

Generally when you post a blog, it's recommended that you tag it with various terms appropriate to the message of the blog. Think of tagging like you would a name tag at a party or networking event and it will start to make much more sense. Generally when you post a blog, it's recommended that you "tag" it with various terms appropriate to the message of the blog. The Wikipedia definition is "a keyword which acts like a subject or category…used to organize web pages, subjects and objects on the Internet." When you think of it this way, what you're really doing is organizing each of your blog posts so that folks can find and search them. By tagging each of them with specific keywords, you'll come up faster when someone searches those keywords. Make sense? Ok, then let's get started learning how to tag. (I promise, it's very easy). You can create two types of tags. You can embed your blog with tags using services like Technorati (more on that in a minute), or you can go to social networking sites and tag your blog as well. I recommend a combination of both.

I talked about social bookmarking in our Blogging Chapter. Social bookmarking is a way of notating favorite sites (i.e., yours) so you can easily share them (via tags) with the Internet community, especially folks who are searching on your search term. I'll explain how to get your site bookmarked, but for now take a look at sites like Digg and Delicious—these are the top two social bookmarking sites you'll want to use.

Okay, here we go. Simple steps to tagging:

1. Create a blog post: Just write your blog, don't worry about doing anything different.

2. Identify some keywords you'll want to use: Just pick some keywords, as many as you want. Don't worry about getting too scientific with this, just be thorough.

3. Create your tags. Most blog platforms now offer tagging suggestions, but if all else fails, use your keywords. Once you input the keywords, make sure the default button is checked at Technorati. Then go to the bottom and click *Generate Code*—this code will get posted right into your blog. (Tip: always post this code at the end of your blog). When you're done, you'll see code in your blog like this: http://amarketingexpert.com/ameblog/?p=289

4. Each of these sites has a different set of criteria for bookmarking your blog post. If you're blogging every day, this might seem pretty tedious. If it's too much work to tag and bookmark each of your posts, handpick a few each week and focus on those. The idea is that you want to get these keywords out in cyberspace so folks can find you.

Red Hot Tip!
Social Bookmarking Made Simple
Simply put, you want to tag each of your blog posts in one or all of the following social networking sites. The one slightly time-consuming piece is that you'll need to set up accounts for each of these will be a bit time consuming, but once you do, it will take you a minute or so per post to add a social bookmarking tag to each of them. Here are some of the most popular social bookmarking sites:

Twitter
Digg
StumbleUpon
reddit
Pinterest
Delicious
Dataswift
Fark
Slashdot
FriendFeed
Newsvine
Diigo
DZone

Blog Feeds

The next step in blog promotion is called an RSS feed. RSS stands for Really Simple Syndication. You've no doubt seen those little orange boxes on websites. These are subscriber feeds—"push" technologies, pushing your content to subscribers and allowing them to follow hundreds of sites without having to visit them individually. It also lets you—the publisher of content—remain visible on the radar screen of your reader/customer. When new content is posted on your site, your subscribers are notified and sent either full versions or summaries, depending on the service they've subscribed to. Thanks to this online syndication, you can subscribe to a variety of websites and every time there's a new entry made, you're notified through whatever service your feeds are submitted to.

RSS Feed Services

There are a variety of feed services that will allow you to syndicate your blog or podcast. FeedBurner (feedburner.google.com) and FeedBlitz.com are probably two of the most well-known and well- respected in the industry. Many blog services have feeds tied into them, but I still recommend listing your feed with a variety of different services. This allows you to tap into any and all feed services your readers subscribe to.

Getting started with these individual feed services is very easy, and once you're in their system the rest is simple, just update your blog and podcast, and subscribers will be notified. By adding this feed service, you're not only able to keep your readers abreast of what you're doing, but it also allows you to track how many subscribers you're getting and manage the list more carefully. Subscribers, regardless of whether they subscribe to your e-zine, blog or podcast, should be handled with care. They've subscribed to you because they feel you have something of value to say, so don't disappoint them. Don't sell out by serving them up random ads or advertorials, unless you're endorsing a product that you feel they could benefit from. Also, keep your content updated as often as possible.

Whether it's a blog or podcast, the key is to stay on their radar screen. While it's not easy to generate new ideas all the time, consider the cost and return of ad placement. In a world inundated with ads, each year they become less and less effective. While it's a lot more work to generate content, the payoff will be much bigger in the end.

Internet specialist Jeniffer Thompson of Monkey C Media says: "Once your RSS feed is working on your site, you have to make it easily accessible to your readers who will then make the choice to subscribe to your feed. This is why services offered by sites like FeedBurner are so valuable to a serious blogger. FeedBurner allows your readers to easily subscribe to your blog while choosing their desired method of retrieval. While some people will choose to receive emails, others may choose to have your new blog posts added to their feed readers like the one offered by Google."

If after reading all this your head is spinning, don't worry. It's not as complicated as it sounds. There are some great tools out there to help make your RSS feed as powerful as possible. But a blog has made this process easy and painless. In fact, most blogs have this already built in, and for others (like WordPress), you can just add a simple plug-in to establish an RSS feed.

THE GOLDEN RULES OF BLOGGING

"The Internet is a giant international network of intelligent, informed computer enthusiasts, by which I mean people without lives."We don't care.We have each other."
— *Dave Barry*

All right, so you have a blog, now it's time to get serious. There are ways to grab traffic and there are ways to lose it. Once you have someone's attention you want to keep it, right? Of course you do. So abide by the Golden Rules of Blogging and don't (inadvertently) show readers the door before you've had a chance to engage them and, of course, sell your product. Also, the idea of having a blog is gaining traffic, yes? These Golden Rules will cover that too, and then some.

1. *Host your own blog.* Why? Because the idea behind blogging is getting traffic, momentum and exposure and all the great benefits of blogging. If you don't have your own URL and your own identity, you're really only using half of your blogging ability. Also, if you utilize a blog platform like let's say Wordpress.org, and you are blogging on something controversial, they can pull you if they don't like it (they don't often do this, but it has happened). Yes, it's free and it's great. You can still use the blogging software but incorporate it and host it on your own URL.

2. *Make your blog unique.* A friend of mine just bought a silver Toyota Corolla. Great car, but it's nondescript. Not that there's anything wrong with being nondescript, but if you apply the same principles to your blog you'll vanish in cyberspace. Get a custom blog or modify it somehow. Don't settle for what the blogging service gives you (standard templates and settings), create your own unique message and look. If you don't have the skill to do this on your own, then hire someone, it'll be worth whatever you pay, and you don't have to pay much. Most highly-customized blogs cost less than $2,000.

3. *Allow people to post or comment on your blog.* All comments and posting should be welcome. Comments mean someone's actually reading your blog and thinks enough of it to talk to you about it. When folks do comment, respond back and let them know you appreciate them taking time.

4. *Check out the competition.* There's a saying about chefs that goes: Even the best chefs eat at other restaurants. Why do they do this? They want to know what the competition is doing. The message here is, read other blogs in your genre. Get to know these bloggers, post on their sites and invite them to blog on yours. Not only will you be able to keep up with the "chatter" out there on your topic, but it's a great way to network.

5. *Watch your tone.* Don't talk down to people. Blogs are conversational—as though you were talking to your reader over a latte. And please, don't talk about yourself. Yes, you can talk about what you're doing, share your life (as long as it relates to your topic), but if you do it all the time it will get boring. It's okay to talk about your product, just remember it needs to be about your reader. Help them, guide them, offer them advice and insight and make your blog worth reading.

6. *Make your blog must be specific.* If your visitor can't tell what your blog is about in the first five seconds of visiting, they'll move on.

Blogging can be fun and is certainly a great way to build your audience. By following these simple rules you'll not only be a better blogger, but able to use this astonishingly easy platform to its greatest advantage.

Mistakes Bloggers Make

Now that you know the Golden Rules of Blogging, here's a list of what not to do. These are some practices that could affect ranking, as well as how "sticky" your blog is!

- Don't use pre-set defaults that come with the blog programs. Create your own brand.
- Don't be too soft-sell. Whenever possible, be controversial or take an unexpected stance on your topic. People love different viewpoints.
- Don't forget to utilize submission tools to submit your blog to directories.
- Don't forget to post often. Frequent posting is key here—you should be posting at least once a week.
- Don't turn your blog into a sales tool. Keep in mind that the blog is meant for informational purposes, not to use as an advertising tool. People will stop reading your blog if you keep filling it with advertisements.

Keeping the Content Churning

All great ideas come with a price. For blogging, it's creating the content as we discussed above. But it doesn't always have to be a grind. Let's take a look at some ideas that should help to germinate several—if not many—new posts.

1. *Industry news* – People in your industry want to know what's going on, and the best way they can find out is by asking an expert: you. So blog on news, trends and industry developments. But don't just relay the information—relay it with your own personal spin. How does this

affect you personally or the segment of the industry you're in? How could it affect others in the same market? Also, don't just keep to industry news. Often global or regional changes will have an effect on your market, so watch for these and blog on them. Then link back to the stories you're referring to, and keep the link-backs going in your blog. Linking to a story that's getting high visibility in the news can only help your blogging efforts.

2. *Other blogs* – If you're not doing so already, you should be monitoring other blogs in your industry and commenting on what others have to say. This is key, especially for virtual networking. You'll want to follow the blogs of industry experts, clients and competitors and be ready to comment, applaud or offer a contrarian view on their topic. Not only is this a good way to stay connected to those in the industry, but many a spirited debate has been born from a blog post. There's no quicker way to drive traffic to your blog then by commenting on someone else's, who is then encouraged to respond (with a link back to your blog, of course).

3. *What are you afraid of?* – Everyone is scared of something, but few of us dare to admit it. One of the quickest ways to endear yourself to your readers and secure reader loyalty is to be real and to offer a voice to a genuine concern or worry. By addressing your biggest fear as it relates to your topic or industry, you're probably tapping into the unspoken fears or hesitations of others. In doing so, you'll pull in an even greater following. This is called "addressing the elephant in the room"—we all see it, but most of us want to pretend we don't.

4. *Books, products or industry inventions* – Be the first kid on your block to try something new or read a newly released book and then blog on it. When I first read *The Long Tail*, it not only inspired a review, it also spawned an entire article on the topic.

Remember, when it comes to blogging the honest, genuine voices get the biggest followings. In the print-on-demand/publishing industry, there was a blogger called POD-y Mouth Girl. She blogged anonymously and though she's since abandoned it, you can still see old posts here: http://girlondemand.blogspot.com/. The blog was funny, biting and irreverent, but regardless of her stance as to print-on-demand, all POD publishers worth their salt would give one of their printing presses to be mentioned on her blog. That's the kind of attention you want.

Another Great Blog Secret

A recent article in *The Wall Street Journal* talked about homeowners expediting the sales of their homes by focusing on aspects that might get overlooked even in a savvy real estate listing. In one example, a woman wrote in her blog about her garden, how much she loved it, how many different types of exotic plants she grew and how proud she was of it. A fellow horticulturalist who wanted to buy a house spotted her blog and immediately put in a bid for her home. This buyer probably never would have been attracted to the standard real estate write-up (3 bedroom dwelling), but the niche focus of the blog drew him in and closed the sale. How does this relate to your product or service? What aspect have you overlooked? Have you zeroed in on all of your micro-niches, or is there a group you're overlooking?

Celebrity Blogging

Ready to become a celebrity blogger? Here's how: If there's a celeb doing something that ties into your topic, blog on it. The more outrageous the celebrity story, the better. If you can hang your star on something that's making celebrity news, do it!

Red Hot Tip!

Now that you're blogging, you may get quoted, referenced and/or excerpted on other blogs. Keep track of all of your mentions by getting Google Alerts. Follow your name, product and blog URL. It's important to track your blog address because some folks might reference a post without mentioning your name.

Feedback and Blog Comments

If you aren't getting people commenting on your blog, don't despair. It takes a while to get folks responding and offering feedback, but the more you can tap into issues your reader cares about, the more comments you'll see popping up on your blog.

PITCHING BLOGGERS

"Microsoft Products are Generally Bug Free."
— Bill Gates

So the art of pitching bloggers is well, an art. Much like the media, they are inundated with pitches, suggested stories and review copies of books. As the Internet keeps getting flooded with new products and services, bloggers are at the receiving end of a lot of new material, most of which they won't even consider. Much like pitching the media, you should treat bloggers like gold. Don't discount them because they don't have traditional airtime. As we've talked about in this book, blogging and the bloggers who run these e-communities can sometimes have more influence than a *Wall Street Journal* reporter.

When it comes to pitching bloggers, think of them as media. As such, you'll get a general sense of the best (and worst) ways to pitch them. Here are a few tips to get you started:

1. *Understand the "blog food chain".* Not unlike traditional media, the bigger the blogger the tougher it is to break in, so be patient and make sure you're pitching a blend of first and second tier bloggers so you don't get discouraged.

2. *Separate the good from the bad.* When it comes to blogs, nearly everyone has a blog now, so how can you find those first, second and third tier blogs while staying away from the "mom and pop" type that can't really further your message? Start with a Boolean search on Google (search

string: "your topic" and "blog") and begin reviewing the various blogs that pop up. Look for frequency in blogging (daily, weekly, etc.), tone, relevancy of material and topics/content addressed. A good way to determine this is in the posting. If the postings are all banter about recipes, family vacations and other personal anecdotes sprinkled in with relevant on-point material, you might want to stay away from these. Why? Because good bloggers stay on-point, which also helps drive traffic to these sites. Bloggers who are just hobbyists and not opinion drivers will differ in their postings and because of this probably won't attract the level of traffic other blogs get.

3. *Know the blog.* Don't pitch randomly: Know the blog and blogger you're going after. This means reading past postings—lots of them.

4. *Personalize your pitch.* Comment on the blog posts they've ran, and never, ever, ever send an unedited form letter.

5. *Keep it brief.* Bloggers don't have a lot of time to cycle through endless text, so make your email easily scannable.

6. *Research the blog posts before pitching.* You want to make sure that while the blog is on topic, they haven't done a story like yours in a while. Yes, it's okay to pitch them a similar topic but not if they already covered it last week. It's likely they won't feature it again unless you can come up with a new angle.

7. *Highlight the benefits early on.* Don't make the blogger scan through your email to figure out why you're pitching them. State your benefits early and as often as necessary. Remember, it's got to matter to their readers.

8. *Be persistent but don't be a stalker.* While I encourage you to send a gentle (and short) reminder email if you don't hear back after a couple of weeks, obsessively emailing the blogger will only get you relegated to their junk mail folder.

9. *Don't send attachments, and don't send your press release.* Bloggers aren't like traditional media. They don't care about the spiffy press release you wrote, so don't include it. If appropriate, you can lift text from it, but save the formal releases for the media.

10. *Free stuff is great, but don't bribe.* If you are promoting a book, bloggers will expect to get a copy so they can review/discuss it. While it's okay to send promotional items, be careful about walking that fine line between promotional swag and bribery.

11. *Become a source.* Once you've tapped into a blog, become a source for that blogger, even if it means turning the blogger onto someone who is more qualified to be their expert. Not every story will be fantastic for you. Don't hesitate to share your leads with the blogger. Try to stay on a blogger's radar screen with relevant tips, insights and news to keep him updated on his (your) industry and help make his own blog cutting-edge.

12. *The mainstream media reads blogs.* If you still aspire to attract traditional media air time, know this: The media reads blogs and will often consider people who are featured on a number of blogs to be experts. Also, some bloggers might be attached to media outlets, which allows them to expand on stories featured in the mainstream media and offer daily updates on particular topics.

13. *Saturate the market.* Bloggers don't need exclusivity, so you can go crazy with your pitches. But remember, the more saturated your category (money, relationships, diet and health, etc.), the tougher it might be to get those crucial bloggers' attention. We addressed doing a mix of first and second tier bloggers, but in these markets you might want to consider focusing on second (or third) tier bloggers first. This will build your reputation and let you catch rising stars and springboard up-tier to more prominent blogs.

14. *Follow the links.* Most of the more popular blogs have links to other similar blogs. Follow those links because they might be worth a pitch as well.

15. *Speaking of links, they rule.* One of the best ways to get a bloggers attention is to link your blog to theirs. Add their blog URL to your blogroll. This small effort carries a lot of weight.

16. *Monitor the blogosphere.* Keep an eye on other blogs by tapping into blog monitoring services like Technorati and Blogdex. This will allow you not only to follow bloggers (who may not have RSS feeds) but also to help you determine how many times your name and product have been featured in one of the blogs you've pitched (bloggers may not always tell you).

17. *Finding news-driven blogs.* While you're searching for topic-related blogs, don't overlook news-driven blogs. These are ones that vary in topic but are driven by daily news items. If you have a story that ties into a hot news topic, these blogs might be the best place for you to go (we've listed a few of them below).

18. *A little gratitude goes a long way.* A good part of marketing is relationship building. Saying "thank you" after your review has been posted, your interview has gone live or your guest blogging event has occurred will go a long, long way.

To give your new blog campaign a kick start, I'll list a few of the major news blogs here. If any of these seem relevant to your campaign, add them to your list of blog media and start following their entries:

- BuzzMachine.com
- Instapundit.com
- The Huffington Post (www.huffingtonpost.com)

- WPCandy.com
- Wired.com
- MSNBC Breaking News (breakingnews.tumblr.com)
- The Economist (theeconomist.tumblr.com)
- Yahoo! (news.yahoo.com)

Blog Carnivals

If you haven't participated in a blog carnival and you've been blogging for a while, then head on over to Blog Carnival and get started. It's super easy. Just find a category/topic that you can speak to or have blogged on and submit those blogs for consideration. It's a great way to virtually network and publish more content online.

Blog Worksheet

This is a sample of a worksheet I use in training sessions. It will help you break down your tasks, give you ideas on what to blog on and (hopefully) put you on a blogging schedule you'll feel you can keep.

Blogging ideas:

- Talk about current news
- Review other products or services
- Interview industry experts
- Talk about your views on current trends
- Address the elephant in the room

My next three blog posts will be on:

1)____

2)____

3)____

Blog check list:

- ✓ Is the title of my blog compelling enough? Does it contain any keywords?
- ✓ Did I spell check my blog post?
- ✓ Did I create tags for each post, using keywords?

Quick blogging tips:

- ✓ Be sure to social bookmark each of your posts through sites like Digg, Stumbleupon, Google Bookmarks and Delicious.
- ✓ Comment on other blog posts—it's a great way to do some virtual networking!

Blogs I'd like to network with (if you don't know specific blogs, list blog topics):

____

____

____

More Blog Directories and Analytics Tools:

Technorati.com
OnToplist.com
Blogdigger.com
Blog Directory (www.blog-directory.org)
Google Trends (www.google.com/trends)
Google Webmaster Tools (www.google.com/webmasters/tools)
StatCounter.com/
Woopra.com/
Piwik.org/

BLOG COMMENTING: A GREAT SEO STRATEGY

"Computers have lots of memory but no imagination."
— Author Unknown

For the past five or so years, we've organized teams to support clients' efforts to increase the SEO of their websites. We've done this a number of ways, but the biggest and most powerful is through blog commenting.

When we first launched teams to offer blog commenting, most people didn't have a clue how powerful this type of marketing was. Most Internet people did and have been doing it ever since. Now it has become more mainstream, and everyone seems to want to jump on the blog commenting bandwagon. But let me caution you, because there's a right way and a very wrong way to do this. I'll explain both.

Creating a Blog Commenting Plan

The first step in blog commenting is to create a plan and, of course, know who you'll be engaging with. To start, decide who to follow—who will become part of your online networking tribe? You want people influential to your industry. They might be competitors or spokespeople. They might also be authorities in one way or another. Whoever they are and whatever they offer, it should somehow dial into what you are promoting. I recommend that you make a list of the top five to ten names. Don't go overboard for now. I'm sure there are more people you could engage with, but to start just focus on a few. You can grow the rest of your list from there.

Once you have your list, start following their blogs and find out where they are appearing. This might mean commenting off of their website (I'll explain in a minute why that's important). First, let's look at how you can organize this information:

RSS feeds – This is the quickest and simplest way to get started. Subscribe to their RSS feeds and keep all of these in your online reader or Google iPage. That way you can spend a few minutes in the morning going through your blog posts to see which ones you want to comment on.

Twitter – This is another great way to find content to blog on. Follow your favorites on Twitter and follow the links to their blogs. This will often give you great insights into the biggest and most popular posts on their website. Don't forget to comment on their Twitter posts, too.

Google Alerts – This is another great system for finding good content to comment on. Plug in the names of the folks you're following and their blog URLs, too. As I mentioned earlier, bloggers will often reference a blog post and not the name of the person blogging, so having this link as one of your Alerts will allow you to follow each and every mention of this blogger. So, why do you want to blog off their site? Anytime a blogger is featured on a website, it's likely that site is one you'll want to follow, too. Or at some point you may also want to blog comment on that site as well. It's a great way to network with folks who might one day interview you or feature your company or product.

Tips for a Great SEO Plan

Frequency: I generally recommend you try to comment on three to five blogs a week. I also suggest you spend no more than 30 minutes a day ferreting through blogs and posting—anything more becomes a time-drain that will prevent you from keeping up this work.

Engagement: Remember that each comment is no different than a post you would write for your own blog. You'd never consider writing "great post!" on your site and leave it at that, right? You should consider writing short but thoughtful posts for your blog comments. Offer additional insight, another perspective or a link to where the reader can get more information. Don't be salesy; that's the first way you'll get blasted.

Quality over Quantity: As per the above note, make it count. Don't worry about the number of posts you make, but spend the time considering the quality of the comment itself. You'll find much better engagement and response when you do.

Where's the Juice?: The SEO juice from this strategy will be apparent in the incoming links that now direct to your site. Each time you post a comment, it will ask you for your URL (if you're already registered on a particular site, the login will remember your URL and post it in each comment). While not all blogs allow follow links, there's a lot of debate on nofollow blogs and whether they are still good for SEO. Nofollow describes sites that block the outbound link to your website, essentially telling Google not to consider your link in its ranking algorithm. Even though you may get referral traffic, Google will act as if you aren't even on the site. Meaning, you may get traffic from the link, but no "link juice" per se. This deters a lot of SEO people, but my take is that if a link from a high-traffic site will get you traffic, why not post there? We still see a significant amount of traffic from links posted on nofollow sites. And keep in mind that search engines pay a lot of attention to social sites like Twitter and Facebook, which are both nofollows. (see here for more on nofollow: http://www.google.com/support/webmasters/bin/answer.py?hl=en&answer=96569.)

The point is, a strong SEO plan should include blog commenting. Not just for the SEO benefits, but for the engagement and connections blog commenting brings with it. Consistent, high quality posts will not only bring you great traffic, but fantastic connections as well.

PART FIVE:

DRIVING EVEN MORE TRAFFIC

"Some things Man was never meant to know. For everything else, there's Google."
— Author Unknown

THE POWER OF VIDEO

"I had a fortune cookie the other day and it said: 'Outlook not so good.' I said, 'Sure, but Microsoft ships it anyway.'"
— Author Unknown

According to We Capture (www.wecapture.co.uk), by 2013 over 90% of Internet traffic will be video-based. When it comes to convincing a consumer to buy, often there is nothing more compelling than a good sales pitch. Yes, you can have excellent packaging and a clever name for your company, but nothing turns a consumer into a buyer quicker than a hefty pitch that pushes every single hot button (including a few they didn't know they had).

Video as a means to promote a product or service is a great sales pitch, but only if it's done right.

Red Hot Did You Know?
Companies who use online video for promotion have seen a sales lift of 20–40% and visitors who view product video are 85% more likely to buy than visitors who do not.

With all the talk today about using video as a promotional tool, it's easy to get caught up in a YouTube-driven world. It's a great idea, certainly, but there's one catch: you've got to make your viewer feel something. When a video about a bullied bus monitor went viral, she wound up with over $600,000 in donations.

The dog being told that all the goodies were gone and "talking into the camera" (http://www.youtube.com/watch?v=nGeKSiCQkPw) became so popular (almost overnight) that within a few days it was all over the mainstream media. That's the impact of video.

Making the Video

Lights, Camera, Action! If you do decide to use video to help promote your message, make sure that it looks professional. Recruiting friends and family to star in your mini film is cheap, but be careful that the outcome does not appear unprofessional and—dare I say—cheesy. It's easy to create bad video, and sadly this could reflect poorly on your message. You may be portraying your product or service in a light that does not do it justice.

Still Images

Still shots, photographs and images can be more powerful than video for some products. The secret is to create movement and action through the use of transitions and video editing techniques. There is a popular technique made famous by documentary filmmaker Ken Burns—it's called the Ken Burns Effect. Here's what Wikipedia has to say: "Burns often gives life to still photographs by slowly zooming in on subjects of interest and panning from one subject to another. For example, in a photograph of a baseball team, he might slowly pan across the faces of the players and come to rest on the player the narrator is discussing."

If you decide to use still photographs, make sure you buy royalty-free images like those found at iStock.com where you can find professional images for as little as $1–3. After you create an account, you can create a "lightbox" in which to save your selections and sift through later. Often the most daunting part of video creation is the hunt for images. It can take hours if not days to find the perfect image, so take your time and spread out the search over several days. Also, be sure to buy the right size. An Internet video is typically 320 x 240 pixels, but you might consider building yours larger so you do not lose resolution when you compress your files. Your images should be around 800 x 600 pixels for use in online videos. Keep in mind, you may want to crop your image, or if you decide to use the Ken Burns Effect you will need a higher resolution to pan across.

Voice

The other component to consider is voice. If you opt to include voiceover you'll need a professional way to record it and an artist whose narrative style complements the tone of your video. The script needs to be simple, yet effective. It's easy to get carried away with a verbose script that becomes very complicated to produce. Consider the visuals and timing as you write. A good rule of thumb is to write a script that will not exceed thirty seconds. Believe it or not, this will usually result in a forty-five second video by the time you add credits and such, which is about the perfect length.

Lastly, you'll need music. While it may be tempting to use your favorite song, this will likely get you into trouble. There are many sites that offer royalty-free music—you may have to credit the artist, but this certainly beats paying royalties or finding a cease and desist letter in your mailbox. If in doubt, ask for permission—not everything is royalty free.

Creating Sticky Video

How do you make a video stick online and gain massive viewing? First, creating a homemade video works, but only occasionally. Sometimes we see video that goes viral and it's been homespun. This is the exception, not the rule. A recent study of Internet users found that 68% of us prefer video that's professionally produced. Second, don't go over 45 seconds. Why? Because attention spans are short online, and regardless of the length of your video users will typically only watch the first 10 seconds of it before they decide to continue watching or move on. So you've got to make those first 10 seconds really count. Don't wait until the end to push the viewer's hot buttons, push them early and often. It could be the difference between a sale and a viewer who merely bypasses your message. Keep in mind, too, that as you're designing your video it's likely the person viewing this hasn't seen your product and doesn't know who you are. Think of movie trailers (sometimes the best parts of the movie) that are designed to entice the audience into seeing the film. Your video trailer should do the same thing. It's another product and another way to capture sales. As a sales tool, these videos can also be used to plug future products or services. Consider the "credits" section at the end of the video to lead readers to new products, pre-orders or wherever you want to send them.

Testimonials on Video

If you're getting good customer feedback from your product, service or book, why not capture this enthusiasm on video? With smaller cameras, phones and digital delivery, creating video testimonials is easier than ever. In fact, if you're eager to build your video testimonial gallery, why not offer customers an incentive for turning their written review into a video? It's easy to create a video page on YouTube, and you can use it to upload your videos.

A Case Study in Video

When video burst on the scene a few years ago I decided to run a test on one of my own books. I took *Candlewood Lake* to a video designer with an outline for how I felt the mini-movie would unfold. Soon my book was coming to life. We added music, made a few final changes and released it into the world. The response was enormous. Within hours of launching this video, we were seeing a serious spike in book sales and hits to the website. Then the emails started pouring in: "Is this book going to be a movie?" (music to any fiction writer's ear), "Where can I get a copy of this book?" (more music) and so on. This small test showed me that video for books, when done properly, can help propel a campaign or even give a boost to an older title. *Candlewood Lake* was almost two years old when we ran this test.

Videos Types for Promoting your Product, Service or Book

Some business owners think about creating videos similar to movie trailers, which are expensive and heavily produced. But you have so many other options available and good reasons for incorporating video in your promotion strategy. Let's explore the components and purposes of each type of online video.

Understanding the facets of these various types will enable you to create the most valuable online video possible.

Trailer

This looks like a movie trailer. It's great for promoting books, but can also work for products and services, too. A video trailer is a short, professionally produced video that highlights the main points and provides just enough of a hook to create a desire to get the whole story. It needs to be done very, very well to convert into sales.

Relationship Videos

Relationship videos are content-rich in nature. Examples of relationship videos include video newsletters and video blogs where you, as the expert, deliver your content in video format. Internet users are becoming increasingly accustomed to reading e-newsletters and blogs—you can take this one step further by constructing videos.

If you are promoting a book, read portions of it (as long as you're good on camera). If you are positioning yourself as an expert, read an article that you've written. With videos, you can create a presence on the Internet and become a celebrity within your market. In addition, many customers are more apt to purchase a product or service when they trust the seller, which equals more sales. Get your smiling face out there to build trust and establish a more personal relationship with your customer.

Website Infomercials

The purpose of an infomercial is to prompt people to take action. These videos motivate customers to opt into your subscription list and/or click on a link to purchase an item or service. This works especially well with special offers—just like you've seen on television. It is critical that your website infomercial cuts to the chase and is only 2–4 minutes in length. This differs from a 30 minute infomercial on television.

You should have a short website infomercial because people tend to have a much shorter attention span on the Internet and are more active. You don't want them to become bored and click away from your website!

How-To Videos

How-to videos are tutorials for your product or service. *Showing* customers how to solve a problem is much more effective than forcing them to read the solution in print. Creating these types of online videos often cuts down on service calls and refund rates. You can determine the content based on your customers' needs. Using a how-to video to cover various help topics or FAQs is a beneficial idea.

CREATING VIDEO THAT GETS ATTENTION

"Three things are certain:
Death, taxes, and lost data.
Guess which has occurred."
— David Dixon

There are many options for promoting your video online. Let's go over a few basics and then we'll put the power in your hands.

We've discussed the types of videos you might want to create, but now let's look at some specific ways to market your video content.

Optimizing Your Videos

Finding the perfect keywords for your video is a great way to gain some additional traction and traffic. It's also a great way to optimize your video for search. Using the links we discussed in an earlier chapter, identify keywords for each video you upload. Think of each video as its own webpage and treat it as such. Video titles, descriptions and tags all get equal search time in Google, so be sure to use them wisely. Let's look at each of these areas separately:

- *Video titles* – Keep your title to no more than sixty characters, because after that it gets cut off. Using the term "video" in the title will help you gain even more traction in Google search results.

- *Video tags* – For this I recommend using the keywords you found for the video. If you have a multi-word keyword, such as "Internet marketing expert," put this in quotes, similar to what you'd do in Google.

- *Video description* – You have a lot of room here with a 5,000 character limit, so feel free to create an enhanced, keyword-rich description.

Viral Video

A misconception with video marketing is thinking that a video will go viral, when that rarely happens. Videos that go viral are either exceptionally funny, tragic or a result of a celebrity on camera (likely doing something they weren't supposed to). However, video promotion can be well-utilized by anyone. But the relationship value of the video along with the fact that you are gaining links from the video sites back to your website means that whether the video goes viral or not is secondary.

Distribution

After you have chosen one of the four formats mentioned earlier (trailer, relationship video, website infomercial or how-to), distributing them to the multitude of video websites provides links back to your website and traffic following those links. As of today there are over fifty different video hosting sites, and that number continues to grow every month.

Here is a list of the ones we like best right now:

BlinkBits.com
Blip.tv
Bofunk.com
Break.com
Buzznet.com
Crackle.com
Dailymotion.com

DropShots.com
LiveJournal.com
LiveLeak.com
Metacafe.com
Bing Video (video.msn.com)
Photobucket.com
Stickam.com
Veoh.com
Google Videos (video.google.com)
Yahoo! Screen (video.yahoo.com)
Viddler.com
Vimeo.com
VMIX.com
WordPress.org
Xanga.com
YouTube.com

Host a Video Contest

We all know video is super popular, but is there a way for you use video to engage your readers? You bet. Besides having one professionally created, you could host a contest that encourages readers to create a short video about you. You'll need to award some great prizes, but think of the fun you could have with a video contest like this. Especially if your product slants to a younger crowd, a video contest could be a great way to promote it while getting your readers engaged in your message. To host a contest, you must register as a YouTube partner. This is a free service and you can find out more at http://www.youtube.com/yt/creators/partner.html.

Red Hot Did You Know?

Did you know that YouTube boasts over 800 million unique users each month? Here are some more eye-popping stats:

- **Over 3 billion hours of video are watched each month on YouTube.**
- **72 hours of video are uploaded to YouTube every minute.**
- **70% of YouTube traffic comes from outside the US.**
- **YouTube is localized in 43 countries and across 60 languages.**
- **In 2011, YouTube had more than 1 trillion views—that's 140 for every person on earth.**

Now that's a lot of viewing!

More Video Promotion Tips

Here are some ways to make the most of your video:

- Put your video on your own website and use it to tell visitors what you want them to do. We did this on our home page at amarketingexpert.com with great results.

- When you pitch the media, insert a link to the trailer in your email. Don't send it as an attachment—an overaggressive spam filter will eat it for lunch.

- Send a sample of your video to every media contact you pitch. Never let a press kit leave your office without a disc or, better yet, put links to your video in your media room and send the media there.

- Got a social networking page? You should. Add the clip or a link to it on the page and be sure to promote it on Twitter, Pinterest, Google+ and LinkedIn.

- Blog about your videos often, especially if you're adding new content to your YouTube page on a consistent basis. No, I'm not talking about repeating a blog over and over, but blog on the successes you've had thanks to your video. Oh, and add a link to the video, too.

- If you are promoting a book and trying to get a signing lined up but have been unsuccessful, let your book speak for itself, literally. Drop off a copy of your book trailer to an as-yet-unconvinced bookstore manager, and I can almost bet you'll get a signing in the store.

- If you're doing an event where you are displaying your product, service or book, bring the video to show while you're there. Our clients who've done this have sold almost twice as much product. The video really pulls in buyers.

- If you're a speaker, start your talk off with a 20–50 second video to "set the stage" for your session.

- Just like you can tell a book by its cover, you can often tell a video by its packaging. Get your CD cover professionally printed—don't skimp on the first impression! In fact, why not have your video burned to a business card-size CD that you can pop into the card slot of a presentation folder?

Red Hot Did You Know?

According to We Capture, 59% of senior executives prefer to watch video instead of reading text and 80% of executives are watching more online video today than they were a year ago.

AUTOMATING YOUR MARKETING

"Life would be so much easier if we only had the source code."
— Author Unknown

Imagine this: You're sitting on a beach in the Caribbean sipping a Mai Tai; while back home your website is selling your products for you without you having to do a single thing. Well, there is one thing. Should you order another Mai Tai, or go with a Rum Punch? Think this can't happen? Well it can. Automating your website and sales tools is the first step to increasing your income. Not just because you're making sales but because it frees you up to do other productive activities to promote yourself and your message.

There are a few ways that you can automate your systems. The first is to have the right e-commerce program, which we discuss in a bit. The second is to have sufficient product that can be generated via an automated system that doesn't require packing and shipping. Our site, for example, is packed with things that the buyer can get immediately, like special reports that are instantly downloadable and audio products that can be listened to right away. The third piece to this is responding to inquiries. If you have a book that is part of a larger business, as mine is, then you'll no doubt be getting queries for business, pricing, etc. A book tends to lend itself to business growth, and so it brings in a lot of new inquiries. Not all of them are right for our services or ready for our marketing packages, so we keep them in the autoresponder system (or, rather, they subscribe to it) and they contact us when they're ready. So your autoresponders would also encourage calls ("Call us for ____"), but really the system is just designed to keep you on their radar screen. When they're ready for your service, product or book, they'll know how to get in touch. I started using autoresponders about eight years ago, and they continue to be a vital component of our marketing system.

What are Autoresponders?

Autoresponders are a way to automate the information you send on a regular basis. For example, you can automate a welcome letter when people subscribe to your ezine, or send a thank you note when someone buys your product, service, book or, as I mentioned above, answer someone's immediate query for pricing or assistance. Ideally, you should try to automate as much of your site as you can, and you can easily accomplish this with autoresponders. Check with your hosting company to see if they offer this. If they don't, there are a variety of autoresponder companies out there.

Red Hot Tip!

Autoresponders we love:
Constant Contact
AWeber
GetResponse.com

Why an Autoresponder?

While autoresponders may not be as sexy as some of the new social media, it should not be overlooked. Here's why: We get flooded with information via text messages, tweets or Facebook status updates—the information is endless. We don't often retain what we read or hear just once. That's why there is the "marketing rule of seven"—it takes seven impressions of your book, message or product for your consumer to take notice. Certainly it's conceivable that you could manually send out email messages to your customer base, but if you're trying to run a business, create new products, sell more services, write new books and all of the other things that fill your day, this really isn't very reasonable.

As your email list starts growing and your followers start multiplying, you want to automate as much as you can. You might not like the idea of automating your marketing because it seems less personal (or, in some cases, like a lot of work), but without a certain amount of automation your marketing will never grow beyond what you can handle in a day. Yes, we all want a personalized experience within the company, and trust me when I say that a certain amount of automation will help achieve that. As an example, we have automation handle all of our newsletter sign-ups. These are folks who come to our website and want to subscribe to our newsletter. They don't need a personalized email, they don't need a call, they just want information. Other people land on the site and want more than just information, and they contact us in a variety of other ways. But the autoresponder that's in place helps to manage the flow of new users that find us. It also keeps us on their radar screen. I created *52 Ways to Sell More Books* for our autoresponder, and we deliver tips, insights and helpful advice in two separate emails.

Understanding How a Good Autoresponder Works

For an autoresponder to be effective it needs to be populated with small bits of information that are delivered sequentially over a period of time. In order to encourage people to sign up for your autoresponder, you must offer them something they need. This is called an "ethical bribe", you give them something to get them to sign up for your newsletter. The autoresponder is very similar: give them something they need so you can get what you need— their email address.

To understand how autoresponders work, think about the last time you subscribed online to a course or event. You gave your email address in order to get something valuable in return. That value was delivered in the form of information, and often this information was not delivered all at one time. A good autoresponder isn't just a one-shot deal; it's a system that drops information one bite at a time into the end user's email inbox.

When I was first introduced to autoresponders I wasn't really sure how to use them. Then I remembered that we are all content creators. At this juncture in our careers we probably have more content in the form of blog posts, Twitter updates and e-books than we ever thought we would. This content has enormous value not just as a whole product, but also as bits and pieces. It's these bits and pieces that we plug into an autoresponder to send out.

The Many Uses of Autoresponders

There are a lot of uses for an autoresponder. As I mentioned, we use it for our email capture. It's our ethical bribe and people love it. But you can use an autoresponder for just about anything. Here are some ways I've seen autoresponders used:

- *Lessons* – E-learning is a fun way to deliver information. You can drop lessons into an email that delivers them right to your customers' inboxes.

- *Exclusive content* – Give your end user access to content not available publicly.

- *Book teasers* – Deliver part or all of your book via autoresponder. That's what I did with *52 Ways to Sell More Books*. I also gave folks the option to buy it now if they wanted to.

- *Tips, wisdom, insight* – Deliver your brilliance on a regular basis.

- *Interviews with experts* – Your consumers might love these interviews. They can be print or video, in which case you'd point them to your YouTube channel.

- *Questions, questions, questions* – Readers love questions, especially the most frequently asked questions you might get.

- *Service inquiries* – These follow-up emails are a bit more focused on the sale.

- *Special offers and sales* – Provide special offers on existing products or services.

- *Follow-ups* – Includes reminders, instructions, etc. for teleclasses and teleseminars.

Timing Your Messages

Before you embark on your autoresponder campaign, create a publishing schedule. My recommendation is to keep the first few emails close together—so immediately when someone signs up they get email #1, then two days later they get #2, and two days after that they get #3. From there I tend to space these out a bit more so that my *52 Tips* can actually spread out over almost three months. Once you get through that first three or four email sequence, I recommend dropping drop back to once every 7–10 days. Remember, you're still connecting with your end users, but you're not staying in their face (and cluttering their email) in some obnoxious way.

Message Length

Autoresponders should be short. Keep them to 200 words or less. Especially when you're delivering frequent content during days 1–4 of your sequencing, you don't want people to have to read a lot. I can almost guarantee you if they do they'll unsubscribe from your list.

How many you should have is entirely up to you. You might talk to some Internet marketers who say you should always be communicating with your end users, but keep in mind the funnel that you're working with. Our autoresponder is the key to our newsletter, which goes out every two weeks. We don't want to inundate them with too much content, so at some point our autoresponder ends but gives the end user the option to restart the sequencing.

Autoresponder No-Nos

Years ago when autoresponders were first used by marketing mavens, they were often used to sell. The autoresponder was part tip and mostly sales pitch. This worked for a while, but I can guarantee you it won't work anymore. These days it's all about content. High quality, helpful advice and great content. Make sure that your autoresponder is 99% helpful or entertaining content and only 1% marketing. In fact we don't even really market in our autoresponder. Instead, we invite folks to contact us for a free 30 minute consultation. Remember the call to action—each autoresponder should have a call to action without being overly salesy. You'll keep your readers a lot longer that way and create a fantastic marketing funnel of loyal and buy-ready followers.

Marketing with Electronic Mini-Courses

Another great use for autoresponders is the electronic mini-course. If you're looking for a novel and powerful way to get repeated exposure to your audience, you might want to consider launching an electronic mini-course. The key is to build trust and offer useful content your reader can benefit from. As you build trust, you're also going to build a readership and a following. This will lead to increased book sales.

In its most basic form, an electronic mini-course is a free how-to information product that contains three to seven lessons from your business. Getting the reader hooked on your book, product or service is what this is all about.

Once you've drafted your lesson plan, you'll want to make sure that your final lesson gives people a reason to buy your book from you. Whether it's through a bonus or other subscriber offer, make sure there's some sort of call to action.

As far as launching your mini-course, start experimenting with autoresponders so you don't have to worry about sending each course individually. You can set up autoresponders to automatically deliver your course in the exact time and format you decide. I recommend launching one course a week, but if you'd rather not have your reader wait a week to get their next course—you can certainly launch one every other day.

Start targeting your mini-course using a subscriber list that you've pulled either from your website, personal appearances or both. Offer your list members a chance to benefit from this free informational tool. You can also ask your web designer to include a link on your website or a pop-up that encourages people to sign up. Once you've started launching your electronic mini-course, get some feedback from your subscribers and continue to improve or add to it as needed.

Email Announcements

A recent *Wall Street Journal* article discussed how email ads are becoming more entertaining and informative to help draw consumers in. While we think that spam is the killer of the email ad, the opposite is true. Many retailers are pouring huge efforts into email ad campaigns, but not just your average ad—instead, retailers are getting creative, fun and informative. You can use this information to your benefit. For example, send around a colorful email ad that offers some holiday tips. Then tell your readers what your product can do for them and why it's the perfect holiday gift. Oh, and one more thing—keep them from being too over-the-top salesy or hard sell, and most of all keep these emails short. People have much less time during the holidays.

Summary

Automated marketing allows you to harness the power of technology to reach more and more potential customers. Spend some time automating your marketing and you will have more time to count your money...or sit in the Caribbean sipping that Mai Tai.

HOW TO INCREASE YOUR NEWSLETTER VISIBILITY BY 100%

"The Internet is just a world passing around notes in a classroom."
— Jon Stewart

Newsletters are a great way to stay in front of your audience, but I'm amazed by how many people still have no idea how to manage their own newsletter. I see sloppy copy or newsletters that haven't been edited (am I really going to buy from someone who doesn't have the time to edit their newsletter or make it look nice?). I also see newsletters that veer off topic so much that I instantly unsubscribe. And my absolute favorite: how on earth did I ever end up with this newsletter in the first place?

If used correctly, newsletters can be a great way to get your message out there, offer helpful advice and keep people in your marketing funnel. We've had our newsletter for ten years, and it's been a solid way to stay in front of our audience and educate them about their market and what we do as a company. Candidly, I might consider getting rid of other things we do promotionally, but never our newsletter. It's often the single biggest business driver to our company. It's not easy—it requires work, but the rewards are tremendous. Here are some ideas for enhancing your newsletter and growing your audience:

- *Know your audience* – While this might sound trite and a bit "duh," it's actually more important than you might think and, ironically, quite overlooked. Many business owners who put out newsletters write more for themselves than for their audience. This is a huge mistake because most of the time your consumer won't care about things the way you do. Speak to their pain, their needs and their hot buttons, and most importantly know exactly who they are before you start cranking out newsletter copy.

- *Other newsletters* – It's important to know what other folks in your industry are putting out there. This will help you learn what you like, what you don't like and what might work for your market. Also, you want to really understand your market space and other experts who share your arena.

Red Hot Tip!

Ready to promote your newsletter? Try these resources:

- **E-ZineZ.com**
- **The Ezine Directory (www.ezine-dir.com)**
- **EzineArticles.com**
- **eZINESearch.com**
- **Published.com**
- **New-List Email Newsletters—a series of mailing lists that provides more than 6,000 subscribers updates on new e-zines. You can even add your own newsletter to the list. (www.new-list.com)**

- *Subject lines* –This is probably the most important part of any newsletter. They need to grab the reader's attention, and if you know what your audience wants, the subject lines shouldn't be hard. But they must speak to the needs of your reader. Of all the things going on in their lives (as it relates to whatever you are selling), what's their biggest need right now? Answer that and you've got a perfect subject line.

- *Who cares?* – Whether it's a newsletter, a blog post or a tweet, ask yourself "Who cares?" If you can identify the person as your reader and the content is important enough to get them to care, then you have a good topic. Remember, it's not about you—in fact when it comes to creating great content and newsletters that rock, you don't matter at all. Keep that in mind, and understand that this is about putting together a message that 100% benefits your reader.

- *Personal notes* – Recently I got an email with the subject line: "A personal request," which prompted me to open it. The email started out "Dear," with a bunch of spaces after the word "dear" because I had not entered my name into their system. Be really careful of this. Not everyone enters their name into your email list when they sign up, and if they don't, these types of emails look a bit odd to the recipient. A subject line that said "A personal request" along with an email that was anything but personal caused me to unsubscribe right away.

- *Length* – A lot of people say that they prefer shorter emails to longer ones. I say it really depends on your market. Our newsletter is pretty long but it's packed with content, and I hear from authors all the time that they keep these issues, often printing them out. Your market will dictate how long or short your newsletter should be, and if you are following others in your market, this will also give some ideas for the ideal length.

- *Colors vs. text* – I'm still a big fan of text-based newsletters. I know that folks will say that color works best, but color newsletters can be harder to read on your phones and often wind up in spam filters.

- *Frequency* – How often you deliver your newsletter will generally depend on your consumer, but a good rule of thumb is once a month at a minimum and once a week at a maximum. I would not recommend sending your end-user too many announcements and newsletters. Keep in mind that these are also a lot of content to create. If you build a loyal following, you can often create special blasts with more frequency and not lose readers, but keep in mind that we're all inundated with so many emails, less is more.

- *Editing* – Please make sure your newsletter is edited, this is so important. Remember that everything is your résumé. I used to know a guy in publishing who put out a newsletter that said "this is not edited." I felt like it detracted from his message to put out a newsletter filled with typos. Not good. If you don't have time to edit your newsletter, you should consider whether or not you have the time for it at all.

- *Appeal to the "skimmers"* – Most people skim email these days, so appeal to them. Use short paragraphs, bullet points and strong headlines. That way your reader can glance through the newsletter without having to sift through endless copy and get to the heart of the information they are looking for.

- *Promote or not?* – I'm not a fan of a newsletter that's all heavy promotion. You know the ones I mean: they scream "Look how fabulous I am" and contain a lot of sales copy and special offers. I unsubscribe from those pretty quickly. Ideally you want to strike a balance. Clearly you are doing this to promote yourself and you want your readers to know what you do, what your message, book or product is and how they can get it. You can and should talk about this in every issue, but a healthy balance is 95% information and 5% sales. You'll build customer loyalty much faster this way.

Having a solid base and a consistent way to communicate with your audience can really help to optimize and increase your bottom line. A newsletter might seem like a lot of work, but in the end if it's done right, it will pay off in some pretty amazing ways.

MOBILE MARKETING MAGIC

"The Internet is full. Go away."
— Author Unknown

The term "mobile" tends to confuse a lot of business owners. Questions pop up like "Do I really need it?", "Is my site mobile ready?" and "What do consumers expect from mobile?" Deciding to go mobile is, for many, no longer an option. With staggering numbers of people accessing content on their mobile phones, having a site that is viewable in mobile is a must. I asked Tania Mulry of DDx Media (www.ddx-media.com) to spend some time breaking mobile down for us.

Q: Why is mobile marketing so important today?

Admit it. Your mobile phone is a remote control for your life. No other form of media can compare to its power in your world. It is your most personal device, and you almost never share it, unlike TVs, radios, newspapers, magazines and computers. Your mobile phone is always on, always with you and most likely, you even sleep next to it!

According to the website Wireless Intelligence, there are over 6.4 billion mobile connected devices in the world as of this writing. Considering the world population just crossed 7 billion, that's pretty amazing. A survey conducted by the Cellular Telephone Industry Association (CTIA) determined that 92% of Americans simply do not leave the house without their cell phones.

Analysts predict that mobile advertising spending will meet and then exceed online advertising spending in the next year. Here's why:

Mobile has enormous potential to connect advertising in the physical world directly to response and commerce opportunities on the phone. Mobile is a bridge that makes advertising more accessible and actionable to each consumer, and therefore it has the potential to increase the ROI of every marketing channel to which it is cleverly connected.

Luth Research and the Mobile Marketing Association surveyed marketing thought leaders on the trends, issues and future direction of mobile marketing and offered these compelling statistics:

- 82% of marketers are using some form of mobile marketing
- 71% of marketers increased their mobile marketing budgets for 2012
- The 79% of respondents using mobile marketing in their loyalty programs are deriving great value
- 51% of respondents state that they receive higher ROI from mobile than traditional marketing programs

One of the most compelling benefits of mobile marketing is that it invites your prospective customer into a very intimate conversation and provokes nearly instant attention and response. Once you are invited into an ongoing mobile conversation with a customer, you have a golden opportunity for high engagement, and if you cultivate that relationship well it can be a fruitful one.

Q: What can be done with mobile marketing? Can you give some examples?

Think of your phone as a mini computer—in fact it is probably better equipped and more powerful than a computer you had 10–20 years ago. This miniature marvel is a tiny gift from the marketing deities because it can help you share so many cool experiences with your audience:

- Sharing exclusive content—pictures, videos, songs, podcasts, voicemails
- Collecting leads and automating follow-up from advertising, trade show exhibits, etc.
- Inserting your branded message in apps, mobile websites, text subscriptions through mobile media placements, which can range from text to static banners to rich, interactive display ads
- Providing optimized content when your consumers search for your type of business through hundreds of mobile search engines
- Welcoming the consumer on your mobile website
- Providing the ultimate, permanent branded experience on your mobile applications

There are so many uses that can pay off for small businesses. Here are some scenarios that drive real return on investment:

- *Capturing leads at tradeshows* – Businesses spend thousands of dollars to exhibit at tradeshows, but come home with a baggie full of business cards and no action plan. By setting up an incentive for tradeshow visitors to opt-in with mobile, web or QR codes and then setting up an automatic follow up sequence with text, email and voice messages, you can pre-qualify these leads and get them scheduled for sales presentations much more quickly and efficiently. This technique can save thousands of dollars of qualification calls and makes it much quicker to capture leads and convert them to sales. This drives the return on investment on any tradeshow through the roof.
- *Mobile commerce* – So many more people are shopping with their phones. Businesses can pick up a piece of that action by creating a mobile commerce app or website. This can be enabled with a full store, order customization, shopping cart and set up of delivery or pick-up service.

This can be a real moneymaker for anyone whose customers are living on the go—restaurants, spas/salons, retailers, those with products to sell, etc.

- *Mobile loyalty* – Building repeat customers is a huge focus for most small businesses. That's because it is much easier to treat your existing customers well and ask them to make more purchases than it is to attract new customers. Now, businesses can create a mobile loyalty program that simulates the "punch card" approach that has been so popular in the past. Every time someone comes in and makes a purchase, the staff can either let the user scan a QR code or enter a secret code into an app to "punch" the card and get the customer excited about coming back for a special offer after a certain number of visits.

Q: What's the number one thing I need to do to make more money with mobile?

Sometimes the simplest things make the biggest difference. Your first order of business when building a mobile marketing strategy is to think of ways you can use existing assets to build your mobile contact database. Mobile calls to action can be added to just about any campaign—print, outdoor, TV, radio, social media, online, events or even banner ads. You can even collect leads from trade shows and events.

Why start here? According to CTIA, nearly everyone is open to text marketing:

- 72% of Americans text message across all demographics

- 77% of customers would like to receive mobile alerts or reminders from companies they choose

- Twice as many people text message than own a television set

When clients first start working with mobile messaging, they wonder if customers will truly read their messages. The answer is a resounding, "Absolutely!"

Because people are so tethered to their phones and use text messaging for urgent conversations with family and friends, nearly all text messages are read within 6 minutes of receipt. Mobile coupons inserted into text messages, therefore, have a 97% open rate and a 20x higher redemption rate than paper coupons! Mobile coupons can be used to increase repeat business, drive revenue spikes on slow days and promote viral sharing of the offer.

According to a study by the International Journal of Marketing, mobile marketing campaigns produced response rates of 31% while email marketing campaigns yielded 6% and print yielded 0.55% response.

According to Gartner, and as reported by CNN, in 2012 over half of the US population (approximately 180,000,000 people) will have used their mobile devices to download coupons and make online purchases. You might as well be sending them something to get them to buy from you.

The most effective form of mobile engagement is through time sensitive special offers or discounts (referred to as mobile coupons). These are most likely to lead to a purchase in store or online (ordering physical products or mobile content such as applications, music, eBooks and games).

Q: Are QR codes really hot? And what gets a better response, text or QR codes or both?

It appears that QR codes are all the rage these days—as their deliciously geeky boxes of black and white pixels are appearing everywhere from billboards to TV to fashion items and packaged goods. QR stands for quick response—and that is a good simple description of what they are meant to do—they are meant to encode simple instructions as a symbol that can be scanned and interpreted by a QR reader. The scanning process drives the user to a specific task on their phone—opening a website, sending a pre-formatted text or email message, calling a phone number or downloading an app.

In a head-to-head test between QR Codes and text instructions, we normally see 3–4 people texting for every person who scans the QR code. It is still a bit clumsy for someone to find the QR code reader on their phone, orient and scan it.

That being said, if QR codes add 25-33% to your response, they are worth including. QR codes are inexpensive to create and manage and don't add to your printing costs.

Q: Is having a mobile site important and how can you easily get one?

The mobile web gets more traffic and engagement than mobile apps. Google/Ipsos's Mobile Movement Study of US consumers in April 2011 found that mobile advertising means business. Of people who react to seeing a mobile ad:

- 42% click on the mobile ad
- 35% visit the advertiser's site
- 32% search for more information on their phone
- 49% make a purchase
- 27% call the business

Despite these conclusive findings, 79% of large online advertisers still do not have a mobile optimized site, according to Google/Kelsey in a 2010 study.

Mobile web traffic is growing tremendously and like the desktop-based web is driven in great part by search. Mobile web users expect content to be relevant to their location, load quickly and be easy to navigate or they are on to the next search result.

Is your business website ready to be found through mobile search? Here's an easy test you can do. Open your website on a mobile web browser. Are there clear action buttons, neatly organized in order of importance to a mobile local searcher? (If so, good job!) Or is it your full website shrunk to fit the screen with big missing chunks? (If so, you really need help!)

I recommend investing in a custom-branded mobile website. There are free and low cost mobile website builders that will convert your content into a decent looking mobile website, but you will have to live with their formatting options, their advertising and limited branding.

Red Hot Tip!
Here are some great mobile website builders:
DDx Media (www.**DDx-Media**.com)
Mobile Roadie (www.**MobileRoadie**.com)
DudaMobile.com
Mobify.com
Mobdis.com
Wapple.net
mobiSiteGalore.com
MoFuse.com
Onbile.com

Q: Do I have to have an app?

I'm often asked by clients if they should focus on building a mobile app or website first. Mobile technology has been converging quickly, and now there are affordable ways to tackle both projects at once for a very reasonable cost.

Successful apps fall into two major categories: they are either extremely useful or extremely entertaining. Ideally, you would want to provide a mix of both factors in any app you launch.

For many businesses, a starting point is to port the essential content you have on your website and social media outlets to a mobile website including your shopping or ordering options. Then identify one or two truly unique, useful or entertaining app-powered features that could make a mobile application a special differentiator for your business. These could be features that tap into the phone's features like the camera, voice or GPS.

Red Hot Tip!

Mobile app design checklist:

- **Start with a concept that allows for regular updates or reasons for return use. Think specials, new product introductions, promotions and a directory of useful words, terms and resources in your market or industry.**
- **Include a social media feature, primarily Facebook, Twitter and Pinterest.**
- **Include features that bring people together. Think sharing, think Words with Friends.**
- **Include feedback elements. Push notifications on your end, bug submissions for users experiencing problems.**
- **Ask users to rate your app after the second or third use, not just when they go to delete it.**
- **Make sure you already have Facebook and Twitter in place.**
- **Use a Tell-a-Friend feature.**
- **Think long-term. Can you create both a useful free and paid version?**

Getting your app published in the popular mobile application stores is a huge rush and it does provide you with a brand new distribution channel to reach a highly engaged, income-qualified target audience. You can give away your app for free to encourage downloads (a great branding strategy), charge for the app or provide a free app and charge for premium content upgrades, so it can also be a new source of revenue for your company.

Once you have your app on your customer's phone, you need to keep them active. Consider these continuity strategies:

Push Notifications

Push notifications are the great wake-up call of the app world. You can send a message to your app customers that will sit and wait on their phones until it is dismissed or viewed. This can be great for reminding customers to open the app to find new surprises. Just beware: overuse this privilege and customers will delete your app or disable push notifications. Keep it infrequent and focused on high value messages for maximum effect.

Loyalty Programs

Create an incentive for your customer to open the app and visit your location frequently. Think of an ice cream shop that offers the tenth cone free and tracks it with a paper punch card. A customer's phone can contain this type of tracking within your app, providing benefits for frequent use.

Dynamic Content

An app should have content that changes frequently: weather, traffic, restaurant specials, blog articles, podcasts, etc. If you are creating content in other channels, have the content automatically sync to your mobile app so that the experience is different every time the app is opened.

Social Media Integration

Collect and display all of your social media accounts in your app, and promote your app using social media. You can also show your YouTube account and gain sign-ups for your email list within your app. All of your efforts in each media channel should be used to drive customers to experience your brand in places they can have a positive experience with it and buy—in your physical store, your e-commerce website or your m-commerce mobile application or website.

Signage / Advertising

Don't overlook the real estate you already own, manage or pay for. Put up signs in your store to promote your apps or mobile messaging program. Add your mobile programs to any ads in local magazines, newspapers or online. Mention it in your print or email newsletter. Talk about it at networking functions. The more mentions of it that you have, the better it will do.

What's Next for Mobile Marketing?

After many years of promising trials, mobile marketing is finally seeing the commercialization of Near Field Communications (NFC). NFC will enable a wide range of innovative consumer experiences. First, we'll be able to create device-to-device content or payment exchanges. Next we'll be able to inspire consumers to use their phones to interact with "smart tags" attached to posters, magazine inserts, in store displays and more so they can enable cool things like downloading music, apps, games, mobile ticketing, mobile payments, entertainment services and couponing. Major phone manufacturers and mobile network operators and popular operating systems are beginning to make pushes in this area.

Any Last Thoughts?

Mobile is a complex area of marketing, and you may want to reach out to an experienced consultant or agency to help you navigate it properly. If you want to get the best results and have control of your campaign, you'll probably want to work with a team that will take your wishes into consideration.

Before you jettison less responsive channels, think of how they can work together with mobile. A print ad or email can invite someone to join your text list with a special incentive, and a mobile text can remind someone to check their email or tune into a radio or TV broadcast. Think of and use mobile messaging as the connective tissue facilitating movement between other channels. That's where the mobile magic lies.

GOING LOCAL: THE IMPORTANCE OF LOCAL SEARCH

"The Internet is becoming the town square for the global village of tomorrow."
— Bill Gates

In our prior chapter, we looked at the important of mobile marketing. Now, it's time to focus in on why it's key to grab your local search real estate.

If your business operates locally, whether it's through an actual storefront or some other means, you'll want to optimize your local visibility. Keep in mind that in order to do this, you'll need to make sure that your website is optimized for local search. This means checking to see if your title tags and meta descriptions reflect local text.

When we think local, we often think of sites like Yelp that allow consumers to review local businesses. Reviews are great but often need to be encouraged. Adding buttons to your website to encourage customers to review you is a good idea. A local dog groomer near me encourages reviews on Yelp by offering five dollars off their next grooming visit when a customer posts a review.

Red Hot Tip!
Get to know your local bloggers and businesses and see if you can get them to link to you from their page. You might have to return the favor, but it'll be worth it. Especially if they are well established, this will really help to enhance your local visibility.

If you're using social media, be sure that these pages are optimized for local as well. Sometimes just adding your city to status updates, tweets, and your About page can be really helpful. In other cases, like with Twitter, you can take advantage of the tools I mentioned in our Twitter chapter to enhance your tweets for local exposure.

I spent some time with Susan Gilbert, who specializes in local search, and asked her a bit more about this important topic:

What is local search?

Local search is when someone "searches" the Internet for a local business or service. It wasn't so many years ago that we would have reached for the Yellow Pages. But today we let our fingers do the walking across our keyboards and mobile devices and search online. A search that includes a location modifier, such as a city name or zip code, is an explicit local search. Examples of local searches include "pest control 98029," "Seattle restaurants" or "doggy daycare San Diego." Local searches often will produce listings with a corresponding map, especially on Google.

Why do local businesses need online marketing?

According to a 2010 Kelsey Group study, nearly all consumers (97%) now use online media to shop locally.

Think about it—what to do if you need a plumber fast? If you live in San Diego and need a plumber, most people will open up their favorite search engine and type in "plumber" plus the name of your town. The listings that rank on the first page of search results will get the most phone calls or leads.

Ratings and reviews impact these listings as well. Therefore, local businesses need to both rank as a top listing and put their best foot forward to get the best reviews. In the Yellow Pages the biggest ad often won, and it continued to do so until the new edition came out next year. With local business online marketing, the goal to rank and have good ratings is a continuing process.

Can you talk to us about Google Places?

As with much of online promotion, Google rules. Google is aggressively marketing against Facebook right now and local businesses offer a leg up on the competition.

Several years ago Google provided every business owner with their own website through an online offering called Google Places. Many local business owners aren't even aware of this and didn't claim their Places page. The Places page is static—not to be confused with a business website—but important to claim and integrate with a business website.

What Google says is important. If you were to search "dry cleaners in Brooklyn," here's how Google will determine the results they deliver:

- *Relevance* – You will only be offered dry cleaners, not unrelated business like coffee shops.

- Prominence – You will be offered the best choices, as determined by SEO, citations, reviews, etc. (we'll talk about citations and reviews in a minute).

- *Distance* – Google calculates how far each dry cleaner is from Brooklyn and offers you the closest locations.

Note: If you don't specify Brooklyn in your search, Google will show you dry cleaners based on your approximate location (as determined by your IP address).

Google algorithm changes (Penguin, Panda)—how does that apply to local search?

The local pages I mentioned recently changed from Google Places to Google+ Local, which is really an extension of Google+. Google forced 150 million businesses that had a Google Places page, which they linked to Google+ Local (called Google Search) to compete with Facebook. These can now be found underneath the *Circles* button in the social site of Google+. Click on the icon that says, *Local* to view more.

Mixed terminology is still in use—sometimes Google's local search functions are called Google Places and sometimes Google Search. If you open up a search window in Google, look at the options on the left starting with *Web* > *Images* > *Maps*. Click on *More* and you will see Places. The red push pins are Google Place listings.

However, if you open a Google Place listing, it now turns into a Google+ account. Here are some of the changes Google made:

Google Places were a static one-page listing with address, telephone number, website and reviews. The new Google+ Local pages are dynamic and interactive—things like *Write a Review* are within a Google+ page now. As people begin to search more from within their Google+ accounts, it becomes all the more important for a business to have a Google Local page.

What are Citations?

Citations are the highly ranked and individually searched listings like Yelp and MerchantCircle. Other factors being equal, businesses with a greater number of citations will probably rank higher than businesses with fewer.

Every local business should have a listing of many different citations like Merchant Circle, Superpages, etc., making sure their name, address and phone number are exactly the same across all of them. If you operate a business but do so out of your home, you cannot use a PO Box or UPS address. Google wants to list local businesses, not work-from-home businesses. If you don't mind listing your home address, then do it. Google doesn't care if the business is in your home. But if you don't want people arriving at your front door, you can get around this by renting a virtual office space to receive your mail or piggy backing onto a similar business and paying them a rental fee to use their mailing address.

There are also industry-specific citations like Healthgrades for medical, Avvo for lawyers and Foursquare for retail.

The searches for local are staggering, aren't they? Can you speak to this?

Today there are well over 10 billion unique searches done each month, and that's just in the United States. Of those searches:

- 30% of queries have local intent
- 30% of all searches contain a city, state or zip
- 82% of local searches result in an offline action
- 50% of offline brick and mortar purchases are preceded by an online search

Also, there are over 53 million smartphones in the US. Mobile Internet traffic is exploding (double-digit monthly growth), and smartphones pull data from local listings

The combination of traditional SEO combined with local listings and citations will bring new and continued customers to local businesses.

Can you explain how reviews are key to local promotion?

Did you know that ninety-two percent of Internet users read product reviews? Reputation management—or the monitoring of and acquisition of good reviews—are critical for a local business to get their phone ringing with new clients. Think about it—would you call a plumber who had three low reviews versus someone who had all great ones?

However, the recent changes to Google have left many business owners feeling bewildered. For instance, in order for a customer to review a business on their Google+ Local page, they must now own a Google account. This means that in some cases local businesses must create a Google account before even beginning the review acquisition process, and the same holds true for a client who wants to leave positive or negative feedback about their experience with a business.

Google purchased Zagat last year, and is now following their 0-3 scale rather than the more typical and prior used 5-star system. A business must have at least 10 reviews before Zagat will score it, and then it ranks that business with a 0 – 30 scale. Whew! How much more confusing can Google make it?

Reviews are available on all the citation sites. Besides being listed on citations, you want to consider how people use these citations when determining who they will do business with. Let's use Yelp as an example. You search for dog groomers + your location. Three have great reviews, the fourth has bad reviews. As a potential customer, which one(s) will you call?

> **Red Hot Tip**
> **Considering local coupons? *Consumer Reports* recently reviewed some of the top locally based coupon apps. See here: http://www.consumerreports.org/cro/magazine-archive/2011/december/shopping/shopping-apps/overview/index.htm**

Does social media play a part in local business rankings?

Social media has become a very big factor today and has huge ramifications. Community and brand matters, and Google is incorporating how social a company is when deciding how they rank in the SERPs (search engine results pages). Google has made it known that the top entities of Facebook, Twitter and now Pinterest will factor into rankings; not to mention Google's run at overtaking Facebook with their Google + accounts—which again plays into the changes they have made to the way business listings are being handled.

What is Map Maker?

Google Map Maker was released in August of 2008 targeting the third world (specifically Africa) and has since then spread to 183 countries. As of April 2011, it has completely replaced Google My Maps and is the dominant mapping facility from Google.

Red Hot Did You Know?

According to a recent survey done by ISACA, 58% of consumers who have smartphones use location-based marketing applications despite concerns about safety and personal information. The survey also reports that the use of location-based marketing apps is up one-third from a year ago.

Here are some other thoughts on local promotion:

- Do you blog, and more specifically, do you blog about local interests? Optimize your posts with local references as well as tags and keywords.

- Are you listed in local directories such as YP.com and SuperPages.com? Check out GetListed.org if you want to see how your business is coming up in local search. This site will also tell you where you should be listed. If you're ready to dig into local, check out this listing from HubSpot on the top fifty business directories for local search: http://blog.hubspot.com/blog/tabid/6307/bid/10322/The-Ultimate-List-50-Local-Business-Directories.aspx

RED HOT RESOURCES

"One of the Internet's strengths is its ability to help consumers find the right needle in a digital haystack of data."
— Jared Sandberg

Books You'll Love

Breitbarth, Wayne - *The Power Formula for Linkedin Success: Kick-start Your Business, Brand, and Job Search* (Greenleaf)

Brogan, Chris - *Google+ for Business: How Google's Social Network Changes Everything* (Que)

Brogan, Chris - *The Impact Equation: Are You Making Things Happen or Just Making Noise* (Portfolio)

Falls, Jason - *No Bullshit Social Media: The All-Business, No-Hype Guide to Social Media Marketing* (Que)

Godin, Seth - *Small Is the New Big: and 183 Other Riffs, Rants, and Remarkable Business Ideas* (Portfolio)

Godin, Seth - *Meatball Sundae: Is Your Marketing out of Sync?* (Portfolio)

Handley, Ann - *Content Rules: How to Create Killer Blogs, Podcasts, Videos, Ebooks, Webinars (and More) That Engage Customers and Ignite Your Business* (Wiley)

Jiwa, Bernadette - *Make Your Idea Matter: Stand out with a better story* (CreateSpace)

Joyner, Mark - *The Irresistible Offer: How to Sell Your Product or Service in 3 Seconds or Less* (Wiley)

Kabani, Shama - *The Zen of Social Media Marketing: An Easier Way to Build Credibility, Generate Buzz, and Increase Revenue* (BenBella Books)

Kawasaki, Guy - *What the Plus! Google+ for the Rest of Us* (Amazon Digital Services)

Kerpen, Dave - *Likeable Business: Why Today's Consumers Demand More and How Leaders Can Deliver* (McGraw-Hill)

Li, Charlene - *Groundswell, Expanded and Revised Edition: Winning in a World Transformed by Social Technologies* (Harvard Business Review Press)

Oddin, Lee - *Optimize: How to Attract and Engage More Customers by Integrating SEO, Social Media, and Content Marketing* (Wiley)

Porterfield, Amy - *Facebook Marketing All-in-One For Dummies (For Dummies (Computers))* (For Dummies)

Safko, Lon - *The Social Media Bible: Tactics, Tools, and Strategies for Business Success* (Wiley)

Scott, David Meerman - *Newsjacking: How to Inject your Ideas into a Breaking News Story and Generate Tons of Media Coverage* (Amazon Digital Services)

Smith, Mari - *The New Relationship Marketing: How to Build a Large, Loyal, Profitable Network Using the Social Web* (Wiley)

Stelzner, Michael A. - *Launch: How to Quickly Propel Your Business Beyond the Competition* (Wiley)

Web Site Designers We Love!

Susan Gilbert, Search Engine Marketing Expert, helping authors *Make More Sales, Create More Buzz, Find More Fans.* www.onlinepromotionsuccess.com

Jeniffer Thompson is the co-founder of Monkey C Media (www.monkeyCmedia.com), a full-service design house specializing in author web sites and book cover design.

Great Training Videos

- How to use Twitter: http://www.howcast.com/guides/588-How-to-Use-Twitter
- How to use Twitter for business: http://www.howcast.com/videos/213774-How-to-Use-Twitter-for-Business
- How to use social bookmarking: http://www.howcast.com/videos/406965-How-to-Use-a-Social-Bookmarking-Site
- How to use YouTube: http://www.howcast.com/guides/589-How-to-Use-YouTube
- How to promote a YouTube video: http://www.howcast.com/videos/396552-How-to-Promote-a-YouTube-Video
- How to use Facebook: http://www.howcast.com/guides/586-How-to-Use-Facebook
- How to use Social Media: http://www.howcast.com/guides/594-How-to-Use-Social-Media
- How to Blog: http://www.howcast.com/guides/583-How-to-Blog
- How to use Google Plus for small business: http://www.youtube.com/watch?v=3N-Jk1zHlmQ
- How to use Pinterest for business: http://www.youtube.com/watch?v=MKQ5MZlgmAs
- How to use LinkedIn for businesses: http://www.youtube.com/watch?v=RbHVUegI1-Y
- Increasing SEO for small businesses: http://www.youtube.com/watch?v=sfb7a7HzjAI

Websites Mentioned in the Book

Search Engine Optimization Sites

www.smartzville.com

www.addme.com

www.freewebsubmission.com

www.submit-it.com

Popular Search Engines

www.Google.com

www.Bing.com

www.yahoo.com

www.Ask.com

www.AOL.com

www.MyWebSearch.com

www.Lycos.com

www.DogPile.com

www. WebCrawler.com

www.Info.com

Search Engine Directory Listings

www. dir.yahoo.com

www. Business.org

www.botw.org

www.DMOZ.org

Podcasting

www.bookmkr.audioacrobat.com

Finding Great Keywords

www.Soovle.com

www. Bing.com

www.facebook.com/bookmarketingame

www.youtube.com/user/BookmarketingAME

www.seomoz.org/blog/beat-google-panda

www.googlefight.com

www.google.com/alerts

www.huffingtonpost.com/penny-c-sansevieri/why-some-authors-fail_b_534629.htm

www. sethgodin.typepad.com

www.Squidoo.com

www.facebook.com/ad_guidelines.php

www.youtube.com/watch?v=ddO9idmax0o

Twitter!

www.Twittonary.com

www.twitter.com/bookgal

www.Nearbytweets.com

www.Twitterholic.com

www.TwitterLocal.net

www.twellow.com/twellowhood

www.TweetStyle.com

www.freetwitterdesigner.com

www.Twitbacks.com

www.twittergallery.com

www.twitter.com/#!/search-home

www.stufftotweet.com

www.dailymashup.com

www.Twitpic.com

www.Twitvid.com

www.foxytunes.com/twittytunes

www.Tweetdeck.com

www. Hootsuite.com

www. SocialOomph.com

ww.twitter.com/#!/petershankman

www.twittercounter.com/pages/twittermail/

LinkedIn

www.toplinked.com/toplinked.aspx

www.linkedin.com/groupsDirectory

www.linkedin.com/static?key=application_directory

Google+

www.support.google.com/plus/bin/request.py?contact_type=hoa_submit

StumbleUpon

www.stumbleupon.com

www.stumbleupon.com/pd/index/redirect-ads

Pinterest

www.pinterest.com/chobani

www.pinterest.com/societysocial/

www.pinterest.com/pulpwoodqueen/

Blogging

www.MyBlogGuest.com

www.BlogCatalog.com

www. DMOZ.org

www.Ask.com

wwwTechnorati .com

www.google.com/blogsearch

www.icerocket.com

www.tumblr.com

www.pingoat.net

www.pingomatic.com

www.kping.com

www. amarketingexpert.com/ameblog/?p=28

www.Slashdotcom

www.reddit.com

www.fark.com

www.friendfeed.com

www.newsvine.com

www.Diigo.com

www.DZone.com

www.feedburner.google.com

www. FeedBlitz.com

www. Wordpress.org

www. girlondemand.blogspot.com

www.BuzzMachine.com

www.Instapundit.com

www.huffingtonpost.com

www. WPCandy.com

www. Wired.com

www.breakingnews.tumblr.com

www.theeconomist.tumblr.com

www.news.yahoo.com

www.OnToplist.com

www.Blogdigger.com

www.blog-directory.org

www.google.com/trends

www.google.com/webmasters/tools

www.StatCounter.com

www. Woopra.com

www.Piwik.org

Video

www.youtube.com/watch?v=nGeKSiCQkPw

www.BlinkBits.com

www.Blip.tv

www.Bofunk.com

www.Break.com

www.Buzznet.com

www.Crackle.com

www.Dailymotion.com

www.DropShots.com

www.LiveJournal.com

www.LiveLeak.com

www.Metacafe.com

www.video.msn.com

www.Photobucket.com

www.Stickam.com

www.Veoh.com

www.video.google.com

www.video.yahoo.com

www.Viddler.com

www.Vimeo.com

www.VMIX.com

www.WordPress.org

www.Xanga.com

www.youtube.com/yt/creators/partner.html

Automating your Marketing

www.Constant Contact.com

www.AWeber.com

www.GetResponse.com

www.E-ZineZ.com

www.ezine-dir.com

www.EzineArticles.com

www.eZINESearch.com

www.Published.com

www.new-list.com

Mobile Marketing

www.DDx-Media.com

www.MobileRoadie.com

www.DudaMobile.com

www.Mobify.com

www.Mobdis.com

www.Wapple.net

www.mobiSiteGalore.com

www.MoFuse.com

www.Onbile.com

www.consumerreports.org/cro/magazine-archive/2011/december/shopping/shopping-apps/overview/index.htm

www. blog.hubspot.com/blog/tabid/6307/bid/10322/The-Ultimate-List-50-Local-Business-Directories.aspx

Twitter Sites

@bookgal

People Magazine @peoplemag

CNN @cnn

The Wall Street Journal @wsj

Harvard Business Review @harvardbiz

BBC Breaking News @bbcbreaking

Time Magazine @time

Good Morning America @gma

Reuters Top News @reuters

Mashable @mashable

CNN Breaking News @cnnbrk

The New York Times @nytimes

Fox News @foxnews

Newsweek @newsweek

The Economist @theeconomist

Fast Company @fastcompany

USA Today @usatoday

CBS News @cbsnews

Us Weekly @usweekly

ABC News @abc

@celebritygossip

@cookbook

@books

Social Bookmarking Sites

www.delicous.com

www.digg.com

www.stumbleupon.com

www.technorati.com

www.reddit.com

Search Optimization Tools

Here are some handy SEO tools for you to try out:

- www.scrubtheweb.com/abs/meta-check.html-Meta Tag Analyzer

- www.urchin.com - Track Your Traffic
- www.linkpopularity.com-Link Popularity
- www.webceo.com-Free search engine optimization tools to optimize, analyze, promote and maintain your site
- www.webconfs.com/similar-page-checker.php-Compare your site to your competition
- www.webconfs.com/search-engine-spider-simulator.php-Spider Simulator (find out what search engines see when they spider your site)
- www.webconfs.com/anchor-text-analysis.php-Back links with Page Rank (see who links back to your site and what their page rank is)
- www.webconfs.com/similar-page-checker.php Similar Page Checker (do you have similar pages that will ding your page ranking?
- www.futurenowinc.com/wewe.htm-Customer Focus Calculator (does your Web site focus on you or your customers.

Security Sites

Your Computer's Security (how secure is your computer?):

SpinRite now brings its legendary data recovery and drive maintenance magic to the latest file systems, operating systems, and hard drives

http://grc.com/default.htm

OSSEC is an Open Source Host-based Intrusion Detection System that performs log analysis, file integrity checking, policy monitoring, rootkit detection, real-time alerting and active response

http://www.ossec.net/

Rootkit scanner is scanning tool to ensure you for about 99.9%* you're clean of nasty tools. This tool scans for rootkits, backdoors and local exploits.

http://www.rootkit.nl/projects/rootkit_hunter.html

Great Places to List Your Event

(whether it's in person or an online event)

- Events and Things to do listed by city: http://www.upcoming.org
- A MTV partnered searchable event listing: http://www.eventful.com
- Helps groups of people with shared interests plan meetings and form offline clubs in local communities around the world: http://www.meetup.com/

Other Helpful Stuff

- **Who's Talking About You?**
- While I love Google Alerts this is one to consider too: www.WhosTalkin.com is a social media search engine. All search results include current mentions on websites, blogs, social media posts, basically anything online. The results are also shown in chronological order, which is often more helpful than Google Alerts which tends to filter out of date results too.
- **Got Blog? Don't forget to add it to**:
    - www.google.com/blogsearch
    - www.technorati.com
- Link Popularity - Know who links to your site: www.linkpopularity.com
- Do you have similar pages that will ding your page ranking?: www.webconfs.com/similar-page-checker.php
- Spider Simulator - Find out what search engines see when they spider your site: www.webconfs.com/search-engine-spider-simulator.php
- Back links with Page Rank - See who links back to your site and what their page rank is: www.webconfs.com/anchor-text-analysis.php
- Fun sites to help you find the perfect Keywords: https://adwords.google.com - http://www.google.com/insights/search/ - http://www.soovle.com/ - http://www.google.com/trends
- www.conduit.com- Free point-and-click toolbar creator

- www.autosenders.com-Free autoresponder
- www.boardtracker.com (coming soon)-Track keywords posted in online forums and message boards.
- www.inboundwriter.com -helps make your content more topical, relevant and compelling to your target audiences, who are more likely to share relevant content with others. InboundWriter also makes content more discoverable on the social web. All of this helps marketers drive better reach, engagement and online conversions.
- www.sitemapdoc.com Free Google sitemap generator
- www.aminstitute.com/headline/index.htm-Headline Analyzer—are you using the best headlines? Check here. Learn if you need to improve your headline to grab people's attention.
- www.debugmode.com/wink -Free software creates PC Videos then streams it on your web site
- www.freeserifsoftware.com/software/PhotoPlus/default.asp- Free Graphics Editor
- www.freeserifsoftware.com/software/WebPlus/default.asp -Free Website Design Software
- www.free.grisoft.com/freeweb.php/doc/1/-Free anti-virus software
- www.zonelabs.com- Free firewall
- www.aplusfreeware.com/categories/util/recovery.html- Data recovery freeware
- www.freefoto.com/index.jsp- Free Photos for your Website
- www.powerbullet.com-Create free presentations in Flash
- www.sourceforge.net/projects/filezilla-Free FTP software for uploading your site to the web
- www.w3.org/MarkUp/Guide-Get Started with HTML
- www.htmlhelp.com/reference/css/quick-tutorial.html- CSS Quick Tutorial
- www.yahoogroups.com Free host for your mailing list

- www.sethgodin.com/ideavirus-Unleash the IdeaVirus, free download
- www.sommestad.com/lm.htm-Manage Creative Ideas with the Literary Machine, free download

Big Media Blogs

Ready to read and pitch some of the biggest blogs in the country? Here's a great list to get started with. Everything from politics to wine to what Britney Spears is doing now, follow the blogs Americans read.

An Obsession With Food (And Wine)

Email: derrick.schneider@gmail.com

Coverage: National

URL: http://www.obsessionwithfood.com/

Focus: This blog focuses on food, cooking and wine. Good variety of posts, blogger also reviews books.

Best of the Web Today

Coverage: National via the Wall Street Journal

URL: http://online.wsj.com/public/search?article-doc-type={Best+of+the+Web+Today}&HEADER_TEXT=best+of+the+web+today

Focus: Best of the Web Today looks at some of the most high-profile news stories from around the world. Keep in mind: if news doesn't fit into a print publication or web site's format or coverage, a journalist may cover it in his/her blog. Email is the best way to send information, as bloggers use the Internet and computer technology to create their blogs.

Blog Herald

Email: editor@ blogherald.com

Coverage: International

URL: http://www.blogherald.com/

Focus: The Blog Herald serves as a premium source of blog and blogging related news for bloggers. Keep in mind: if news doesn't fit into a print publication or web site's format or coverage, a journalist may cover it in his/her blog. Email is the best way to send information, as bloggers use the Internet and computer technology to create their blogs.

Blogging About Incredible Blogs

Email: leebow@gmail.com

Coverage: National

URL: http://bloggingaboutblogs.blogspot.com/

Focus: This blog focuses on blogs and technology. It's a great blog packed with info on the blogosphere.

Blogspotting

Email: (three's an online contact form)

Coverage: National

URL: http://www.businessweek.com/the_thread/blogspotting/

Focus: Business & Finance > Business - News & Media > Media

Technology > Internet - Blogspotting follows the collision of Business, the Media and Blogs. Great insight, great blogs. Definitely a must-read!

Booklust

Email: gpstorms@rogers.com

Coverage: National

URL: http://storms.typepad.com/

Focus: Books, publishing, also does book reviews. Booklust is a blog devoted to books, often rounding up reviews of new books and discussing news surrounding authors, publishing companies and best-seller lists.

Books, Inq.

Email: fwilson@phillynews.com

Coverage: National

URL: http://booksinq.blogspot.com

Focus: Arts & Entertainment > Arts > Book Reviews -Professional Services > Publishing Industry - Books, Inq. follows the world of a Book Review Editor, as well as offering reviews and news about Literature.

Buzz Machine

Email: jeff@buzzmachine.com

Coverage: National

URL: http://www.buzzmachine.com/

Focus: Jeff Jarvis blogs about media and news at Buzzmachine.com. He is associate professor and director of the interactive journalism program at the City University of New York™ new Graduate School of Journalism. He is consulting editor of Daylife, a news startup. He writes a new media column for The Guardian.

CultureVulture

Email: gamesblog@gmail.com

Coverage: International

URL: http://blogs.guardian.co.uk/culturevulture/

Focus: This blog offers a steady flow of gossip, music, movie, TV & radio and book reviews and general culture news from the Guardian's Guide team.

emdashes

Email: emdashes@gmail.com

Coverage: National

URL: http://emdashes.blogspot.com/

Focus: Emdashes is a blog focusing on a variety of topics including books, restaurants, journalism and other topics as they appear in the magazine the New Yorker. The blog is not legally bound to the New Yorker, but uses its articles and information as a jumping-off point. The author is a former book critic for the New Yorker.

Entrepreneurs

Email: entrepreneurs@aboutguide.com.

Coverage: National

URL: http://entrepreneurs.about.com/

Focus: Resources, tips, trends and links to help existing and aspiring entrepreneurs.

GalleyCat

Email: galleycat@mediabistro.com

Coverage: National

URL: http://www.mediabistro.com/galleycat/

Focus: This blog looks at news in books and the publishing industry.

Girl in the Locker Room

Coverage: National

URL: http://www.girlinthelockerroom.blogspot.com/

Focus: Girl in the Locker Room follows how Women are making an impact all over the world. Packed with "girl talk" and book reviews this might be another great blog to go after.

Pop Candy

Email: wmatheson@usatoday.com

Coverage: National

URL: http://www.usatoday.com/blog/popcandy/

Focus:

Pop Candy is a daily Entertainment Weblog covering Entertainment news, Music, Movies, Television and Celebrities.

Instapundit.com

Email: pundit@instapundit.com

Coverage: National

URL: http://www.instapundit.com

Focus: One of the highest rated blogs on the 'Net! This blog takes a look at the worlds of Politics, International News, Government Issues and Technology.

Internet Marketing Strategy

Email: sally@meritusmedia .com

Coverage: National

URL: http://www.proactivereport.com/

Focus: Falkow offers news and views about Internet marketing strategy to look at how technology is influencing marketing and PR. Great blog, very good insights on Internet trends, marketing and future predictions.

Literary Saloon

Email: blog@complete-review.com

Coverage: National

URL: http://www.complete-review.com/saloon/

Focus: This blog looks at current literature and publishing news.

Long Tail

Coverage: National

URL: http://longtail.typepad.com/the_long_tail/

Focus: The Long Tail is a blog focusing on current events and issues in politics, government, and American culture from a writer at Wired Magazine.

MarketingVOX News

Email: editorial@marketingvox.com

Coverage: National

URL: http://www.marketingvox.com/

Focus: MarketingVox follows Media news and trends to help those in the Marketing Industry.

Old Hag

Email: theoldhag@oldhag.com

Coverage: National

URL: http://www.theoldhag.com

Focus: Old Hag is a blog focusing on stream of conscious thoughts on books, media, pop culture and out of the ordinary news briefs. The bulk of the content is geared towards book news, reviews and discussion. The blog has been featured in the Scotsman, Village Voice, New Yorker, and Washington Post.

Book Blogs We Love

These blogs are packed with insights, news, and some critical opinions on what's hot and what's not in publishing.

- Blogcritics: Books http://blogcritics.org/books/
- Reading Matters http://kimbofo.typepad.com/readingmatters/
- MoorishGirl http://www.moorishgirl.com/
- The Happy Booker http://thehappybooker.blogs.com/the_happy_booker/
- Book Fetish http://www.bookfetish.org/
- Booksquare http://www.booksquare.com/
- The Elegant Variation http://marksarvas.blogs.com/elegvar/
- Edward Champion's Return of the Reluctant http://www.edrants.com/
- Readers Read http://www.readersread.com/
- Blog of a Bookslut http://www.bookslut.com/blog/
- Beatrice http://www.beatrice.com/
- Buzz, Balls and Hype http://mjroseblog.typepad.com/buzz_balls_hype/
- Book Ninja http://www.bookninja.com/
- Maud Newton http://www.maudnewton.com/blog/
- Tales from the Reading Room http://litlove.wordpress.com/
- The Litblog Co-op http://lbc.typepad.com/
- Book Dwarf http://www.bookdwarf.com/
- Paper Cuts (New York Times) http://artsbeat.blogs.nytimes.com/category/books/
- Jacket Copy (Los Angeles Times) http://latimesblogs.latimes.com/jacketcopy/
- USA Today Books http://www.usatoday.com/life/books/default.htm
- The Millions http://www.themillionsblog.com/

Mom Blogs

Since Mommy blogs are such a huge influence online I thought I'd include them here in case your topic is Mom-worthy!

- Top Mom Blogs: http://www.topmommyblogs.com
- MomBlogNetwork: http://www.lifetimemoms.com/
- The Mom Blogs: http://www.themomblogs.com
- Parents Bloggers Network: http://www.parentbloggers.com
- CaféMom: http://www.cafemom.com
- WorkItMom: http://www.workitmom.com
- ModernMom: http://www.modernmom.com
- The Mommy Blogger Directory: http://mommybloggerdirectory.com/

Social Networking Bonanza!

Remember when I said there were zillions of (niche) social networking sites out there? I wasn't kidding. Each of these sites is listed by category. Have fun!

Business Networking & Professionals

- www.AdvisorGarage.com - an online directory of advisers who are willing to assist budding entrepreneurs.
- www.ArtBreak.com - an artist community for sharing and selling artwork.
- www.CompanyLoop.com - An online co-working community for global businesses.
- www.DoMyStuff.com - A good site for working professionals looking to find online assistants.
- www.doostang.com- An invite only career community for professionals.
- www.iKarma.com - a specialist in providing customer feedback for organizations and professionals.
- www.ImageKind.com - is a community and marketplace for professional artists.
- www.Jambo.net - lets you connect with your neighborhood friends.
- www.Jigsaw.com - An online business card networking directory for users to establish contacts with each other. Each business card is listed with an email id and a contact number.
- www.Lawyrs.net - A professional social networking community for lawyers.
- www.Linkedin.com - a professional social networking website for business users, one of the most popular such sites out there. Some aspects of it are free, but many are paid.
- www.Mediabistro.com –is for professionals in content or creative industry.

- www.Ryze.com - A site for establishing new connections and growing networks. Connections for jobs, building career and making sales.
- www.Spoke.com - offers access to business network of over 40 million people worldwide.
- www.bayspire.com- WebCrossing Neighbors provides a private label social network with personal spaces and user groups.
- www.XING.com - a networking directory of business contacts powering relationships between business professionals allowing users to connect with each other.

Family

- www.CafeMom.com - a social networking site for mothers to connect and share thoughts with each other.
- www.blogoscoped.com/family/ - Family 2.0 helps you create your own family social network, you can add family members, send personalized emails and create event alerts.
- www.Famster.com - a private secure social network for family members.
- www.Geni.com - an exciting social networking site enabling members to create their family tree.
- www.familytree.com-Although it is a relatively new site, it has grown tremendously fast, and has hundreds of thousands of users.
- www.Genoom.com - creates a meeting place for its site users. They can create a family network by inviting their relatives and discover their past memories.
- www.Kincafe.com - an ideal social network for families to connect with their beloved ones.
- www.Kinzin.com - an online meeting place for families to share family events, photos, stories, and recipes.
- www.babycenter.com- Meet other parents. Share your photos. Get helpful advice

- www.Minti.com - a collaborative parenting site.
- www.myfamily.com - an excellent way to connect with your family members.
- www.OneGreatFamily.com - an online shared database with combined knowledge and data at a single place.
- www.OurStory.com - enables users to share stories of their families with others.
- www.TheFamilyPost.com - a sharing network for communication with family members.

Friends

- www.43things.com - a tagging based social networking site. Users create accounts and list a number of goals or hopes and these are parsed based on similarity to goals of other users.
- www.Amitize.com - a worldwide friendship network.
- www.ASMALLWORLD.net - a private online community designed for individuals who would like to connect, re-connect to share similar thoughts with each other.
- www.Badoo.com - a dynamic multi-lingual social networking site with innovative photo and video features that allows its users worldwide to gain an instant mass audience and interact both locally and globally.
- www.Bebo.com - a hugely popular site (especially in the UK), and similar in philosophy to MySpace. It allows users to communicate with their friends in multiple ways including blogging, sending messages and posting pictures.
- www.Faceparty.com - a UK based community social networking website. It started for youngsters but has now risen to popularity among all age groups.
- www.Friendster.com –a popular global social network for finding new friends and developing friendships as well as searching old friends.

- www.hi5.com - a prominent social networking service in India with over 40 million users. However, Hi5 has recently experienced an upsurge beyond India and has shown increasing popularity in EU too.
- www.Lovento.com –allows you to discover news friends and also find information about latest events.
- www.Multiply.com –a social networking website providing easy way to share digital media which includes photos, videos and music.
- www.MySpace.com - an interactive social networking website consisting of personal profiles, blogs, groups, photos, music and videos. It's currently the biggest social networking site out there, and while it might not be the most advanced one, the users seem to love its simplicity.
- www.Netlog.com - a social community of more than 20 million young Europeans.
- www.Orkut.com - a social networking service owned by Google. It enables users to meet new friends and create communities.
- www.ProfileHeaven.com - a UK based social networking site for teenagers.
- www.reunion.com - a leading online service for discovering old friends, classmates and family members.
- www.Xanga.com - one of the biggest social networking platforms with features of sharing photos, photos and videos.
- www.XuQa.com - an online college social networking site with poker gaming features.

Hobbies & Interests

- www.ActionProfiles.com - social networking community for sports and action.The features of the website are profiles of users with photographs and videos, reviews of products and job discussion boards.
- www.ARTslant.com - a community that provides a dynamic community experience by providing extensive listing of exhibitions, events and openings.

- www.greenmountain.com - At Green Mountain, we hold ourselves to the highest standards in terms of how we run our business and interact with our customers and the community, as well as the impact we have on the environment.
- www.beRecruited.com - beRecruited is a dedicated online community for sport persons and coaches.
- www.CarGurus.com - an automobile community website enabling users to post car reviews, photos and share opinions.
- www.Change.org - a nonprofit social networking website that connects like minded users and allows them to exchange information.
- www.changingthepresent.org - a nonprofit fund raising community with membership of over 400 nonprofits.
- www.ChickAdvisor.com - a sharing community for women users.
- www.CircleUp.com - one of the best community website connecting users to groups, clubs for knowledge sharing, information exchange.
- www.coRank.com - a rating community for users to share interesting information on internet.
- www.DailyStrength.org - a huge community of over 500 groups dealing with health issues and various medical challenges.
- www.Dundoo.com - enables users to create image collages out of social networking profile. A big amount of ads on the site somewhat diminishes the overall impression.
- www.Flixster.com - a community for movie lovers.
- www.FuelEmpire.com – (coming soon) brings automobile enthusiasts together at one place.
- www.Greenvoice.com - an online networking platform for people who are conscious about the environment, who want to inform each other on environmental issues and create a difference.
- www.iYomu.com - an adult social networking website and it allows users to search for site members who have similar interests or for business needs.

- www.Motortopia.com - community for automobile lovers. It consists of passionate lovers of bikes, planes, cars and boats etc.
- www.datemypet.com - is the leading online dating website created exclusively for pet lovers.
- www.uniteddogs.com - a social networking website for dog owners. The dog owners can create profiles of their dogs, create blogs and share their thoughts.
- vSocial.com - Under Construction a video based social networking platform allowing content owners, site operators to deliver the message online with video.

Media

- www.Fotki.com - a photo sharing http://en.wikipedia.org/wiki/Photo_sharing service enabling users to connect with friends.
- www.Fotolog.com - a big online photo sharing community.

Music

- www.bandchemistry.com/ - Under Construction a network for musicians uniting music bands all over.
- www.ihiphop.com - Brings Social Networking and Rich Media Content to the Hip Hop Community
- www.MOG.com - an online community powering site members to discover music and music lovers.

Mobile

- www.Mobango.com - a mobile community service powering users to search for user generated music content, videos and other data.
- www.Mozes.com - enables members to connect & socialize with each other through mobile phones.
- www.Peepsnation.com - allows users with similar interests to connect with each other on location basis.

- www.Socialight.com - a mobile based social networking site where users share their travel experiences with other mobile users.
- www.Wattpad.com - A mobile phone social networking platform allowing users to discover, read and share their stories with each other.

Shopping

- www.etsy.com- Etsy is the marketplace we make together. Our mission is to reimagine commerce in ways that build a more fulfilling and lasting world.
- www.gilt.com- An interior designer community enabling users to post items for sale and for exchange.
- www.bringsome.com - s a global goods delivery platform enabling community members to assist each other with access to best items from across the world.
- www.boxedup.com - users add their favorite products to their list and share it with others.
- www.MyItThings.com - a user generated magazine for shopping.
- www.MyStore.com - is a social market place for buyers and sellers.
- www.Productwiki.com - a common place for users to share information about consumer products.
- www.RedFlagDeals.com - Canada's most popular shopping community, which offers huge discounts to site users.

Students

- talentcircles.com - created to assist college students, alumni with professional opportunities.
- www.College.com - an online community for college students.
- www.CollegeClassifieds.com - is the most recognizable college targeted classified service on the web.
- www.Graduates.com - a social networking site assisting graduate school students to stay in touch post completion of course.

- www.Half.com - leading student market place for buying and selling textbooks at discounted prices.
- www.reflectnow.com - the best place for up and comers to get feedback and exposure, exchange ideas, find new fans, and further their musical endeavors in realtime.
- www.Quizilla.com - a social network for young teens.
- www.RateMyProfessor.com - connects students aspiring to study similar courses by assisting each other.
- www.Student.com - Student.com is a big online community for college students, high school students, and teens with around 1,000,000 members.
- www.StudentSN.com - a social network allowing users to create home pages with contact information, personal information, and photo albums.
- www.Uloop.com - allows students to trade textbooks, promote community events and do host of other activities.

Travel & Locals

- www.Citizenbay.com - a user community for discovering local information.
- www.CouchSurfing.com - a global travel network connecting travelers with local communities.
- www.patch.com- Source for local knowledge you can't live without.
- www.iloho.com - an online travel community with similarity to social bookmarking services like digg.
- www.matadornetwork.com- s an independent media company and nexus of travel culture worldwide.
- www.OurFaves.com - a community of urban savvy folks who enjoy the Toronto city and find out cool places to hang out at.

- www.Rummble.com - enables users to discover as well as share places of interest in your neighborhood.
- www.TravBuddy.com - a cool site for sharing travel experiences, finding new travel friends or reading travel reviews of fellow friends.
- www.Travellerspoint.com - an international meeting point for worldwide travelers.
- www.tribe.net - connect with people for finding a restaurant, a killer apartment, a gentle dentist or a hiking friend.
- www.Triporama.com - provides an easy way to plan and collaborate on group trips.
- www.WAYN.com - WAYN is a social networking website uniting world wide travelers.
- www.wikitravel.org - is dedicated project for creating a trusted, up-to-date travel guide. It has over 16,641 travel destination guides maintained and written by Wikitravellers from around the world.

Just for Fun

- Warp and distort images http://www.debugmode.com/winmorph/
- Free Forum Avatars (didn't you always want to be a singing cat?) http://www.avatarsdb.com/
- Beat Writer's Block with some fun http://www.afunzone.com/
- What Does Your Hero's Name Look Like in Chinese Characters? http://www.chinesenames.org/

- Bored? Create your own caricature http://www.magixl.com/heads/poir.html
- Spice up Your Writing with 1001 free fonts http://www.1001freefonts.com/

SPECIAL RED HOT BONUS

Thanks for buying the latest edition of Red Hot Internet Publicity.

As a "thank you" we've got some gifts for you.

Actually many, many gifts to help you continue to accelerate your promotion!

Ready to grab your goodies? Just scan this QR code in your phone and it'll take you straight there!

Wishing you Red Hot Success,

Penny & Everyone at Author Marketing Experts, Inc.

INDEX

C

D

Q

R

CPSIA information can be obtained at www.ICGtesting.com
Printed in the USA
LVOW07s1958180713

343560LV00019B/969/P